A NEW STYLE ITALIAN GRAMMAR

GUIDA ALLE STRUTTURE DELLA LINGUA ITALIANA

&

VOCABULARY LISTS BY TOPIC

LEONARDO ORIOLO

LONDON 1990

Alla memoria di mio padre

Links Publications 1990

ISBN I 872793 00 2

Links Publications
Centre Two Ossian Mews
London N4 4DX
UK

INTRODUCTORY NOTE

This book is best used in conjunction with the companion volume "Pronti ... Via! The Italian Handbook" which provides essential practice material in easily accessible form. The New Style Italian Grammar can however also stand in its own right as a concise reference guide to the fundamental structures of the Italian language.

It is intended primarily for those learning Italian who are already familiar with a number of basic expressions, enabling them to have an elementary conversation in Italian. The learning method assumed here is that the student gains some conversational confidence, and then begins to look in more detail at the grammar.

As far as young learners of school age are concerned, the guide should not be seen as a list of grammatical rules which have to be digested. Instead it should offer support during the phase of enquiry which follows the realisation that some errors seriously interfere with effective communication. The book helps the student to impose some logical order upon the disparate pieces of language which have been absorbed as a result of communicative activities. The layout is clear and makes learning easier.

The basic content has been derived in the main from the practical developments encouraged by the Council of Europe, resulting in the "Threshold Level" or, for Italian, "Livello soglia". It uses the same classification of levels as the syllabuses prepared for the General Certificate of Secondary Education used for pupils aged sixteen and over in the English school system, namely 'basic' and 'higher'. In particular the vocabulary and situations listed in the syllabus of the Northern Examining Association have helped to keep to a minimum the body of notions and functions used as examples, whilst dealing with the maximum number of practical structures.

For students who want to explore beyond the range of notions and functions listed in the Threshold Level and the subsequent school syllabuses this book provides a framework of grammatical analysis. The analysis aims to take account of the way in which living language is put to use as a real communicative tool by speakers and writers of Italian. The systems of rules outlined in the different sections of this guide, and the extensive vocabulary listed by topic and settings, provide the basis for the learner's continuous development of communicative abilities.

I should like to thank all those colleagues who have tried out some of the material, and who have suggested improvements. My gratitude also goes to Maria Galasso, Maria Pia Oliver and John Broadbent for their advice and encouragement. My students also have been extremely helpful and supportive - both those from the European School and from the courses organised by the Italian Consulate. Finally I should like to thank the editor and staff of Links Publications. Emanuela Agni dedicated many hours not only to entering the text into the computer but also to elaborating the layout of the book. Special thanks are due to the editor, Clive Mira-Smith who made the present publication possible and used it to launch the new Pronti Via! series of Italian teaching materials.

Leonardo Oriolo
March 1990

CONTENTS

15. VOCABULARY LISTS BY TOPIC

1. Nouns (Nomi)

1.1 Gender, Singular and Plural

	Singular	Plural	Ending	
Masculine	ragazz**o**	ragazz**i**	**-o**	**-i**
Feminine	ragazz**a**	ragazz**e**	**-a**	**-e**
Masculine Feminine	getton**e** canzon**e**	getton**i** canzon**i**	**-e**	**-i**

1.2 Common Irregular Nouns (singular-plural)

SINGULAR	PLURAL	
		(a) Some nouns don't change in the plural. They are:
il film	i film	- most words of foreign origin;
lo sport	gli sport	
il re	i re	- monosyllables;
la città	le città	- nouns stressed on the final vowel;
l'università	le università	
la radio	le radio	- some feminine nouns ending in **-o;**
la foto	le foto	
il brindisi	i brindisi	- nouns ending in **-i.**
il ciclista	i ciclisti	(b) The few masculine nouns ending in **-a** form the plural in **-i.**
il clima	i climi	
il turista	i turisti	
il problema	i problemi	
il telegramma	i telegrammi	
		(c) Be careful how you spell the nouns ending in:
lo zio	gli zii	**-io** (when the **i** is stressed, the plural is **-ii**);
lo st**u**dio	gli studi	**-io** (when the **i** is not stressed, the plural is **-i**);
la spi**a**ggia	le spiagge	**-gia** (when the **i** is not stressed, the plural is **-ge**);
la f**a**ccia	le facce	**-cia** (when the **i** is not stressed, the plural is **-ce**);
la bug**i**a	le bugie	**-gia** (when the **i** is stressed, the plural is **-gie**);
la farmac**i**a	le farmacie	**-cia** (when the **i** is stressed, the plural is **-cie**);
l'amico	gli amici	**-co/-go**
l'asparago	gli asparagi	(their plurals are formed in two different ways:
il cuoco	i cuochi	-ci/gi; -chi/ghi). If in doubt use the dictionary;
l'albergo	gli alberghi	
l'amica	le amiche	**-ca/-ga**
la collega	le colleghe	(their plurals are formed as - **che/ghe**);
il dito	le dita	(c) Remember these irregular nouns.
l'uovo	le uova	
la mano	le mani	

Continued ➡

1.3 Common Irregular Nouns
(masculine-feminine)

Masculine		Feminine
lo studente	*student*	la studentessa
il dottore	*doctor*	la dottoressa
il professore	*teacher*	la professoressa
l' attore	*actor*	l' attrice
lo scrittore	*writer*	la scrittrice
il pittore	*artist*	la pittrice
il maschio	*male*	la femmina
l' uomo	*man*	la donna
il celibe	*bachelor*	la nubile
il marito	*husband*	la moglie
il padre	*father*	la madre
il fratello	*brother*	la sorella

1.4 Common Compound Nouns
(singular-plural)

Singular		Plural
l' altoparlante	*loudspeaker*	gli altoparlanti
l' arcobaleno	*rainbow*	gli arcobaleni
l' aspirapolvere	*vacuum cleaner*	gli aspirapolvere
la banconota	*banknote*	le banconote
il cacciavite	*screwdriver*	i cacciavite
il capolavoro	*masterpiece*	i capolavori
la cassaforte	*safe*	le casseforti
il cavatappi	*corkscrew*	i cavatappi
il cavolfiore	*cauliflower*	i cavolfiori
la ferrovia	*railway*	le ferrovie
il francobollo	*stamp*	i francobolli
il marciapiede	*pavement*	i marciapiedi
il passaporto	*passport*	i passaporti
il portacenere	*ashtray*	i portacenere
il portafoglio	*wallet*	i portafogli
il salvagente	*lifebelt*	i salvagente
il sottopassaggio	*subway*	i sottopassaggi

Vocabulary

albergo *hotel*
amico *friend*
brindisi *toast*
bugia *lie*
canzone *song*
ciclista *cyclist*
città *town*
clima *climate*
re *king*
collega *colleague*
cuoco *cook*
dito *finger*
faccia *face*
uovo *egg*
farmacia *pharmacy*
foto *photo*
gettone *token*
mano *hand*
ragazzo *boy*
spiaggia *beach*
studio *study*
università *university*
zio *uncle*

2. ARTICLES (ARTICOLI)

2.1 Definite: (the) il, la, ...

	SINGULAR		PLURAL			
MASC.	il	ragazzo	i	ragazzi	il/i	before a consonant
	lo	studente	gli	studenti	lo/gli	before s + consonant or z
	l'	albero	gli	alberi	l'/gli	before a vowel
FEM.	la	ragazza	le	ragazze	la/le	before a consonant
	l'	aula	le	aule	l'/le	before a vowel

2.2 Indefinite: (a, an) un, una, ...

2.3 Partitive articles: (some, any) del, della, ...

	SINGULAR		PLURAL			
MASC.	un	ragazzo	(dei	ragazzi)	un	before a consonant or a vowel
	uno	studente	(degli	studenti)	uno	before s + consonant or z
FEM.	una	ragazza	(delle	ragazze)	una	before a consonant
	un'	aula	(delle	aule)	un'	before a vowel

e.g.

masculine	il ragazzo	*boy*	i ragazzi	un ragazzo
	il libro	*book*	i libri	un libro
	il supermercato	*supermarket*	i supermercati	un supermercato
	lo studente	*student*	gli studenti	uno studente
	lo specchio	*mirror*	gli specchi	uno specchio
	lo zio	*uncle*	gli zii	uno zio
	l'albero	*tree*	gli alberi	un albero
	l'orologio	*watch*	gli orologi	un orologio
feminine	la ragazza	*girl*	le ragazze	una ragazza
	la studentessa	*student*	le studentesse	una studentessa
	la zia	*aunt*	le zie	una zia
	l'aula	*classroom*	le aule	un'aula
	l'isola	*island*	le isole	un'isola

☞ ***Lo, gli** and **uno** are also used in front of the very few words beginning with **x, pn, ps, gn** and the semi-consonant **i**: lo xilofono (xylophone), uno pneumatico (tyre), lo psicologo (psychologist), gli gnocchi ('gnocchi'), lo iogurt (yogurt). In colloquial Italian this rule is followed less strictly, particularly in front of **pn** and **gn**: un pneumatico, i gnocchi.*

☞ ***Gli** may be apostrophised only in front of **i** (although used less and less frequently nowadays): gli indirizzi/gl'indirizzi (addresses), but gli alberghi (hotels), gli occhi (eyes).*

☞ *The partitive article follows the rules of the definite article: del sale, dell'olio, dello zucchero, dei broccoli, degli spinaci, della frutta, dell'insalata, delle banane, (some, any - salt, oil, sugar, broccoli, spinach, fruit, salad, bananas).*

3. ADJECTIVES (AGGETTIVI)

3.1 Regular Formation

	SINGULAR	PLURAL	Ending	
MASCULINE	ross**o**	ross**i**	**-o**	**-i**
FEMININE	ross**a**	ross**e**	**-a**	**-e**
MASCULINE AND FEMININE	verd**e**	verd**i**	**-e**	**-i**

e.g. Un ombrello rosso. *A red umbrella*
Una penna rossa. *A red pen*
Un ombrello verde. *A green umbrella*
Una penna verde. *A green pen*

3.2 Agreement

NOUNS		ADJECTIVES
Claudio	è	timido.
Claudio e Mario	sono	timidi.
Carla	è	timida.
Carla e Lucia	sono	timide.
Carla e Mario	sono	timidi.
Carlo e Lucia	sono	timidi.

The adjective agrees in gender and number with the noun it qualifies.

An adjective is given in the masculine plural form if it refers to several nouns of different gender.

3.3 Position of Adjectives

☞
- Adjectives usually follow the noun:
  Un libro noioso. Una camera singola. *A boring book. A single room.*
- Sometimes the adjective may be placed either after or before the noun in which case its meaning is often changed according to its position:
  È un uomo grande. *He's a big man.* È un grand'uomo. *He's a great man.*

3.4 Common Irregular Adjectives

Bello and **buono** in front of masculine nouns become:

SINGULAR	PLURAL
bel ragazzo	bei ragazzi
bell'albero	begli alberi
bello zaino	begli zaini
buon ragazzo	buoni ragazzi
buon uomo	buoni uomini
buono studente	buoni studenti

Bello follows the rules of the definite article.

In the singular **buono** follows the rules of the indefinite article. The plural is regular.

☞ The feminine of **bello** and **buono** is regular: bella ragazza; belle ragazze; buona ragazza, ...

VOCABULARY
albero *tree*
bello *beautiful, lovely, handsome*
buono *good*
ombrello *umbrella*
penna *pen*
ragazzo *boy*
rosso *red*
timido *shy*
uomo *man*
verde *green*
zaino *rucksack*

3.5 Demonstrative Adjectives (Aggettivi Dimostrativi)

3.6 (this) questo, ...

	Singular	Plural	
Masculine	**questo** libro	**questi** libri	this; these
Feminine	**questa** penna	**queste** penne	this; these

3.7 (that) quello, ...

	Singular	Plural	
Masculine	**quel** libro **quello** studente **quell'** albero	**quei** libri **quegli** studenti **quegli** alberi	that; those
Feminine	**quella** penna **quell'** isola	**quelle** penne **quelle** isole	that; those

Questo	indicates a person or thing	close to the speaker.
Quello		far from the speaker and from the listener.
Codesto		close to the listener.

☞
- ***Codesto, codesta, codesti, codeste*** *(that, those) are mainly used in Tuscany or in bureaucratic language.*
- *The adjective* ***questo*** *can take an apostrophe in front of a vowel: Quest'inverno (this winter); quest'estate (this summer).*
- *You may sometimes find* ***sta*** *instead of* ***questa****: Stamattina = questa mattina (this morning); stasera = questa sera (this evening).*

3.8 POSSESSIVE ADJECTIVES (AGGETTIVI POSSESSIVI)

MASCULINE		FEMININE		
SINGULAR	PLURAL	SINGULAR	PLURAL	
mio	miei	mia	mie	(my)
tuo	tuoi	tua	tue	(your) informal
Suo	Suoi	Sua	Sue	(your) formal
il suo libro	i suoi libri	la sua penna	le sue penne	(his/her)
nostro	nostri	nostra	nostre	(our)
vostro	vostri	vostra	vostre	(your)
loro	loro	loro	loro	(their)

3.9 Use of possessive adjectives before terms for family relationships

☞ The articles **il** and **la** are not used in front of possessive adjectives referring to relations: **mio** padre *my father*, **sua** madre *his/her mother*, **vostro** fratello *your brother*, **nostra** sorella *our sister*, **tuo** marito *your husband*, **mia** moglie *my wife*, ...

☞ The article is used in front of the possessive adjective only if the relations are:
- in the plural: **i miei** fratelli *my brothers;*
- qualified by a suffix: **il mio** fratellino *my little brother;*
- accompanied by another adjective: **il mio** fratello maggiore *my eldest brother;*
- referred to using a term of endearment: **la mia** mamma *my mum*, **il mio** babbo *my dad.*

☞ The article is always used before the possessive adjective **loro**:
il loro figlio *their son*, **i** loro figli *their sons.*

- *The possessive adjective is normally preceded by the definite article.*
- *Possessive adjectives are used less frequently in Italian than in English.*
- *The gender and number of the possessive adjective agree with the accompanying noun and not with the possessor as in English:*
  Questo è il suo libro e questa è la sua penna [di lui]. (This is his book and this is his pen.)
  Questo è il suo libro e questa è la sua penna [di lei]. (This is her book and this is her pen.)

3.10 Indefinite Adjectives (Aggettivi Indefiniti)

3.11 (every, some, any) ogni, qualche, qualsiasi

	Singular	
Masculine/Feminine	**ogni**	every, each
	qualche	some, any, a few
	qualsiasi/qualunque	any, every

e.g. **Ogni** volta che vado al mare, incontro Andrea. *Every time I go to the seaside, I meet Andrea.*
Ci vediamo tra **qualche** giorno. *We'll see each other in a few days.*
Qualsiasi/qualunque ristorante va bene. *Any restaurant will do.*

- ***Ogni, qualche, qualunque, qualsiasi,*** *are only used as adjectives, never as pronouns.*
- *They are invariable and used only in the singular.*

3.12 (every, no, ...) ciascuno, nessuno

	Singular	
Masculine	**ciascuno**	every, each
	nessuno	no, any
Feminine	**ciascuna**	
	nessuna	

e.g. **Ciascuno** studente deve fare i compiti. *Every student has to do his homework.*
Non ha dato **nessuna** risposta. *He gave no answer.*

- *They take the feminine and are used only in the singular.*
- *They follow the rules of the indefinite article: ciascun libro, ciascun'amica, ciascuno studente, ciascun amico, ciascuna studentessa.*

Continued 

3.13 (other, much, ...) altro, molto, ...

	SINGULAR	PLURAL	
MASCULINE	**altro**	**altri**	other, another, more
	molto	**molti**	much,many, a lot
	parecchio	**parecchi**	a good deal of, quite a lot of
	poco	**pochi**	little, few
	tanto	**tanti**	so much, a lot of
	troppo	**troppi**	too much, too many
	tutto	**tutti**	all
FEMININE	**altra**	**altre**	
	molta	**molte**	
	parecchia	**parecchie**	
	poca	**poche**	
	tanta	**tante**	
	troppa	**troppe**	
	tutta	**tutte**	

e.g. Verrò un **altro** giorno. *I'll come another day.*
Hai **molti** amici italiani? *Do you have many Italian friends?*
È da **parecchio** tempo che non vedo Luca. *I haven't seen Luca for a long time.*
Ci siamo fermati **pochi** giorni. *We stayed there a few days.*
Ha **poca** esperienza. *He has little experience.*
Ho comprato **tanti** libri. *I bought a lot of books.*
Ho preso **troppo** sole. *I caught too much sun.*
Ho rivisto **tutti** gli amici. *I saw all my friends again.*

They take the feminine and are used both in the singular and plural.

3.14 (some, any, ...) alcuno

Alcuno, alcuna, alcuni, alcune (some, a number of, any, no, ...):

- in the singular follow the rules of the indefinite articles and are used only in the negative form: Non ha **alcun'**amica con cui parlare. *She has no friend to talk to.*
- in the plural they mean the same as **qualche**:
  Vorrei comprare **alcuni** libri su Pisa (= qualche libro su Pisa). *I'd like to buy some books on Pisa.*

3.15 INTERROGATIVE ADJECTIVES (AGGETTIVI INTERROGATIVI)

Che?	What? Which?
Quale?	Which?
Quanto?	How much?

3.16 **Che** is invariable and equivalent to **quale, quali**:
Che (=quale) film vuoi vedere? *What film would you like to see?*
Che (=quali) fiori ti piacciono? *Which flowers do you like?*

3.17 **Quale** varies in the plural (**quali**):
Quale materia preferisci? *Which subject do you prefer?*
Quali materie preferisci? *Which subjects do you prefer?*
Quali libri hai letto? *Which books did you read?*

3.18 **Quanto** is variable (quanto, quanta, quanti, quante):
Quanto zucchero vuoi? *How much sugar do you like?*
Quanta frutta hai comprato? *How much fruit did you buy?*
Quanti anni hai? *How old are you?*
Quante materie studi? *How many subjects do you study?*

3.19 COMPARISON (GRADI DI COMPARAZIONE)

3.20 Comparative

più ... di	**(più ... che)**	**more ... than**
meno ... di	**(meno ... che)**	**less ... than**
(tanto) ... quanto **(così) ... come**		**as ... as**

e.g. Ha **più** dischi **di** lei. *He has more records than she has.*
Carla è **più** giovane **di** lui. *Carla is younger than he.*
Lui è **meno** giovane **di** Carla. *He's older than Carla.*
Lei è giovane **quanto** Carla. *She's as young as Carla.*
Lei è giovane **come** Carla. *She's as young as Carla.*

☞ **Più/meno ... che** is normally used when the comparison is between:

- two adjectives:
  Quella poltrona è più comoda che pratica. *That armchair is more comfortable than practical.*
- two verbs or two adverbs:
  È **meno** divertente andare a ballare **che** andare al cinema. *Dancing is less enjoyable than going to the cinema.*
  Lui legge **più** velocemente c**he** correttamente. *He reads more quickly than correctly.*
- in front of a noun or pronoun but only if they are governed by a preposition:
  Perché Daniela è **più** arrogante con me c**he** con voi? *Why is Daniela more arrogant with me than with you?*
  Angela ha scritto **più** lettere a Luca c**he** a Pietro. *Angela has written more letters to Luca than to Pietro.*

☞ In the comparison of equality, **tanto** and **così** are optional and often omitted except when the comparison is between two adjectives:
Nicoletta è t**anto** furba **quanto** intelligente. *Nicoletta is as cunning as she is intelligent.*

Continued 

3.21 Superlative

RELATIVE	**il più...**	the most...
	il meno ...	the least...
ABSOLUTE	**-issimo**	very...

e.g. Lui è **il più** simpatico **di** tutti i tuoi amici. *He's the most pleasant of all your friends.*
Lui è **il meno** simpatico **di** tutti i tuoi amici. *He's the least pleasant of all your friends.*
Lui è simpatic**issimo/molto simpatico.** *He's very pleasant.*

☞ The relative superlative is formed by placing the definite article before **più** or **meno**.
Sometimes the prepositions **tra** or **fra** may be found instead of **di**:
È la **più** simpatica **fra** tutti. *She's the most pleasant of all.*

☞
- The absolute superlative is usually formed by adding -**issimo/a/e/i** to the root of the adjective or by placing adverbs of quantity (**molto, tanto, assai** , ... = very) in front of the adjective:
  Loro sono **molto** simpatici = sono simpatic**issimi.**
- The absolute superlative is also formed by means of a prefix (**arci-, stra-, sopra-, super-, pluri-, ultra-**) or by repeating the adjective:
  Arcinoto (very well known); **stra**ricco (extremely rich).
  È una camera piccola piccola. *It's a very small room.*
- There are also many idiomatic forms of the absolute superlative:
  Stanco morto (dead tired); ubriaco fradicio (as drunk as a lord); pieno zeppo (packed full); ricco sfondato (rolling in wealth); innamorato cotto (infatuated).

3.22 Irregular Comparison

Some adjectives have two comparative forms (the irregular one derives from the Latin):
Questa pizza è buonissima = questa pizza è ottima. *This pizza is excellent/very good.*

	COMPARATIVE	RELATIVE SUPERLATIVE	ABSOLUTE SUPERLATIVE
buono *(good)*	più buono/**migliore** *(better)*	il più buono/**il migliore** *(the best)*	buonissimo/**ottimo** *(very good)*
cattivo *(bad)*	più cattivo/**peggiore** *(worse)*	il più cattivo/**il peggiore** *(the worst)*	cattivissimo/**pessimo** *(very bad)*
grande *(big)*	più grande/**maggiore** *(bigger)*	il più grande/**il maggiore** *(the biggest)*	grandissimo/**massimo** *(very big)*
piccolo *(small)*	più piccolo/**minore** *(smaller)*	il più piccolo/**il minore** *(the smallest)*	piccolissimo/**minimo** *(very small)*
alto *(high)*	più alto/**superiore** *(higher)*	il più alto/**il superiore** *(the highest)*	altissimo/**supremo** *(very high)*
basso *(low)*	più basso/**inferiore** *(lower)*	il più basso/**l'inferiore** *(the lowest)*	bassissimo/**infimo** *(very low)*

4. ADVERBS (AVVERBI)

The adverb is the word that specifies the meaning of a verb, an adjective or another adverb.

e.g. Può parlare **lentamente**? *Can you speak slowly?*
È un ragazzo **molto** intelligente. *He's a very intelligent boy.*
Parli troppo **velocemente**! *You speak too quickly!*

4.1 Formation of Adverbs

In general

☞ Most adverbs (indicating manner) are derived by adding the suffix -**mente:**
- to the feminine singular of adjectives in **-o:**
  Lento-lentamente (slowly), libero-liberamente (freely).
- to the singular of adjectives in **-e**:
  Veloce-velocemente (quickly), breve-brevemente (briefly).
- to adjectives in **-le/-re** (leaving out the **-e**):
  Facile-facilmente (easily), regolare-regolarmente (regularly).

☞ There are also adverbs (indicating quantity) that have a form identical to that of a few masculine singular adjectives: **troppo** (too; too much), **molto** [(very) much; a lot)], **tanto** (so; so much), **poco** (little; not much), ...

☞ Finally there are adverbs (indicating place or time) that have a form not derived from other words: **qui/qua** (here), **lì/là** (there), **mai** (never), **adesso** (now), **dove** (where), ...

4.2 Position of Adverbs

They are usually placed:

- after the verb: Puoi ripetere **chiaramente**? *Can you repeat clearly?*
- before the adjective: **Lei** è **molto** simpatica. *She's very nice.*
- between the auxiliary and the verb in compound tenses: È **già** partito. *He's already left.*

4.3 Classes of Adverbs

- **Manner** (answering the question 'how?'):
  facilmente, lentamente, raramente (rarely), ...
- **Place** (answering the question 'where?'):
  qui, lì, laggiù (down there), sotto (below), sopra (above), ...
- **Time** (answering the question 'when?'):
  adesso (now), oggi (today), domani (tomorrow), prima (before), dopo (after), ...
- **Quantity** (answering the question 'how much?'):
  molto, poco, troppo, abbastanza (enough), ...

Continued 

4.4 Adverbial Phrases

In Italian, it is quite common to find expressions formed from two or more words, acquiring the meaning of an adverb.

e.g. **All'improvviso** (suddenly, **poco fa** (a little while ago), **nel frattempo** (in the meantime), **d'ora in poi** (from now on), **poco per volta** (a little at a time).

4.5 Comparison of Adverbs

☞ Some adverbs (mainly those of manner and a few of time and place) can be made into comparatives and superlatives (see 3.20, 3.21): lentamente, più lentamente, lentissimamente (slowly, more slowly, very slowly).

4.6 Irregular Forms

	COMPARATIVE	SUPERLATIVE
bene *well*	meglio *better*	benissimo/ottimamente *very well*
male *badly*	peggio *worse*	malissimo/pessimamente *very badly*
poco *little*	meno *less*	pochissimo *very little*
molto *very; a lot*	più *more*	moltissimo *very much*

- *The adverb is invariable: lei legge molto. (She reads a lot); lui è molto simpatico (He's very nice); loro sono molto simpatici (They are very nice).*

- ***Qui, qua** = here ; **lì, là** = there. **Qui** and **lì** indicate a more precise location than **qua** and **là**.*

5. Personal Pronouns (Pronomi Personali)

	Subject	Direct Object stressed	Direct Object unstressed	Indirect Object stressed	Indirect Object unstressed
I	**Io** invito	invitano **me**	**mi** invitano	spediscono a **me**	**mi** spediscono
you	**tu**	**te**	**ti**	**te**	**ti**
he; it	**egli (lui); esso**	**lui**	**lo**	**lui**	**gli**
she; it	**ella (lei); essa**	**lei**	**la**	**lei**	**le**
we	**noi**	**noi**	**ci**	**noi**	**ci**
you	**voi**	**voi**	**vi**	**voi**	**vi**
they	**essi (loro)**	**loro**	**li**	**loro**	**gli**
they	**esse (loro)**	**loro**	**le**	**loro**	**gli**

e.g. **Io** invito Emilio e Lisa. *I'm inviting Emilio and Lisa.* - subject
Invitano **me**. *They're inviting me.* - stressed direct object
Mi invitano. *They're inviting me.* - unstressed direct object
Spediscono un libro a **me**. *They send a book to me.* - stressed indirect object
Mi spediscono un libro. *They send a book to me.* - unstressed indirect object

5.1 Subject:

Io (I); **tu** (you 'informal'), **Lei** (you 'formal'); **egli/lui** (he); **ella, lei** (she); **esso, essa** (it);
noi (we); **voi** (you); **essi, esse, loro** (they).

- The personal pronoun is normally used for the subject when it is necessary to emphasise who is carrying out an action.
  e.g. Vado al mercato. *I'm going to the market.*
  Io vado al mercato, tu resti a casa. *I'm going to the market, you stay at home.*
- In the polite form of address when talking to a person (man or woman) with whom one is not on familiar terms, **Lei** is used followed by the verb in the third person singular.
  e.g. Tu parli italiano? *Do you speak Italian?* - informal
  Lei parla italiano? *Do you speak Italian?* - formal
- **Egli, ella** usually refer to people and are often substituted by **lui, lei.**
- **Ella** is almost never used. It can be found in literature or bureaucratic language.
- **Esso, essa** refer mainly to objects or animals and are often substituted by **lui, lei.**
- **Essi, esse** refer to people, animals or objects and are often substituted by **loro.**

5.2 Stressed/unstressed direct object and stressed indirect object:

me, mi (me); **te, ti** (you 'informal'); **La** (you 'formal'); **lui, lo** (him); **lei, la** (her); **lo, la** (it);
noi, ci (us); **voi, vi** (you); **essi, esse, loro, li, le** (them).

5.3 Unstressed indirect object:

mi (to me); **ti** (to you 'informal'); **Le** (to you 'formal'); **gli** (to him); **le** (to her);
ci (to us); **vi** (to you); **gli** (to them).

- **Gli** more and more often substitutes **loro,** which is used mainly in formal situations and in the written language.
  e.g. Gli spediscono i libri = Spediscono loro i libri. *They send the books to them.*

Continued 

5.4 Use and Position of Personal Pronouns

☞ **Stressed forms** (which emphasize the pronoun) generally follow the verb and are used:
- for the direct object: Invitano me.
- for the indirect object, preceded by a preposition: Spediscono un libro a me.
- in comparison: È più giovane di lei. *He's younger than she.*
- in exclamations without a verb: Povero me! *Dear me!*

☞ **Unstressed forms**, (which emphasize the verb), generally precede the verb and are used:
- for the direct object: Mi invitano.
- for the indirect object, without a preposition: Mi spediscono un libro.

☞ **Unstressed** (or conjunctive) personal pronouns follow the verb to make, with the exception of **loro**, one single word:
- with the infinitive: Vengo a prenderti. *I'll come to get you.*
- with the gerund: Scrivendogli ha risolto il problema. *Writing to him solved the problem.*
- with the imperative: Telefonagli subito! *'Phone him at once!;* Telefona loro! *'Phone them!*
- with the past participle: Consegnatagli la lettera, uscì. *After handing him the letter, he left.*

☞ **Unstressed personal pronouns** follow the adverb **ecco** to make one single word (eccolo, eccola, eccoli, eccole, ...): Dov'è il libro? **Eccolo**. *Where is the book? Here it is.*

5.5 Personal Pronouns and the Apostrophe

In front of a vowel the pronouns:
- **lo** and **la** generally take an apostrophe: Non l'ho visto. *I haven't seen him;*
- **mi, ti, ci, vi** may take an apostrophe:
  M'ha già detto che non verrà = Mi ha già detto che non verrà.
  He has already told me that he won't be coming.

5.6 Personal Pronouns and the Past Participle

When the past participle is accompanied by the verb **avere**, it must agree with the direct object pronouns: **lo, la, li, le.**

e.g.

(libro)	L'ho comprato in Italia.	*I bought it in Italy.*
(penna)	L'ho comprata in Francia.	*I bought it in France.*
(libri)	Li ho comprati in Svizzera.	*I bought them in Switzerland.*
(penne)	Le ho comprate in Austria.	*I bought them in Austria.*

5.7 Combined Pronouns

- When necessary, the unstressed pronouns can be combined; in this case direct object pronouns follow the indirect object pronoun.
- **Mi, ti, ci, vi** change to **me, te, ce, ve** when followed by **lo, la, li, le, ne**:
  (Io) Ti spedisco il libro = **Te lo** spedisco. *I'll send it to you.*
  (tu) Mi spedisci le fotografie = **Me le** spedisci. *You'll send them to me.*
  Ve ne impresto due. *I'm going to lend you two of these.*
- **Gli** and **le** change to **glie-**, when followed by **lo, la, li, le, ne (glielo, gliela, glieli, gliele, gliene)**: Glielo dirò domani. *I'll tell it to him/her/them tomorrow.*

5.8 Relative Pronouns (Pronomi relativi)

che	who, whom, which, that
cui	whom, which
il quale (la quale, i quali, le quali)	who, whom, which, that
chi	he who, him who...

5.9 Che is invariable and can:

- only be used as subject or direct object;
- be substituted by **il quale, la quale, i quali, le quali**:
  Ho conosciuto un ragazzo che (= il quale) abita a Varese. *I met a boy who lives in Varese.*
  Ho conosciuto una ragazza che (=la quale) abita a Milano. *I met a girl who lives in Milan.*
  Le ragazze che (=le quali) hai conosciuto sono inglesi. *The girls that you met are English.*
  La torta che abbiamo mangiato, era molto buona. *The cake we ate was very nice.*

5.10 Cui is invariable and can:

- be used as indirect object (preceded by a preposition):
  Ecco il libro di cui ti ho parlato. *Here's the book I told you about.*
- be substituted by **il quale, la quale, i quali, le quali** in indirect object (preceded by a preposition+the definite article): Ecco il libro del quale ti ho parlato.
- be preceded by the definite article (**il cui, la cui**, ...= whose):
  Quel ragazzo, il cui nome non ricordo, è italiano.
  That boy, whose name I don't remember, is Italian.

5.11 Il quale is variable and is used:

- as subject (more formal than **che**):
  I ragazzi i quali (=che) vinceranno la competizione andranno in Italia.
  The boys who win the competition will go to Italy.
- rarely as direct object:
  Le ragazze le quali (=che) hai conosciuto sono inglesi. *The girls that you met are English.*
- quite frequently as indirect object (preceded by a preposition+the definite article):
  Il treno con il quale (= con cui) ho viaggiato era molto veloce.
  The train by which I travelled was very fast.

5.12 Chi is invariable and is only used in the singular. It refers to people. It is equivalent to **colui che** (he who), **colei che** (she who), **la persona che** (the person who), **coloro che** (they who, those who, ...):
Chi ha già il biglietto può entrare. *Whoever has got a ticket can go in.*
Coloro che hanno già il biglietto possono entrare. *Those with a ticket can go in.*

5.13 Interrogative Pronouns (Pronomi Interrogativi)

chi ?	who?
che (cosa)?	what?
quale ?	which?
quanto ?	how much?

e.g. **Chi** ha telefonato? *Who 'phoned?*
Che cosa hai detto? *What did you say?*
Quale dei due preferisci? *Which of these two do you prefer?*
Quanto costa? *How much is it?*

5.14 Chi? is invariable and is used for people or animals:

Chi non ha mangiato il dolce? *Who hasn't eaten the cake?*
Chi ha rotto il vaso? *Who broke the vase?*

5.15 Che? is invariable and is used for objects (it is equivalent to **che cosa**? or **cosa**?):

Che (cosa) avete comprato? *What did you buy?*
(Che) cosa vuoi fare? *What would you like to do?*

5.16 Quale? varies in the plural (**quali**) and is used for people, animals or objects:

Quale di questi vestiti compreresti? *Which of these dresses would you buy?*
Di queste parole quali conosci? *Which of these words do you know?*

5.17 Quanto? is variable (**quanto, quanta, quanti, quante**) and is used for people, animals or objects:

Quanto le devo? *How much do I owe you?*
Quanta ne desidera? *How much would you like?*
Quanti verranno alla tua festa? *How many are coming to your party?*
Quante sono venute alla tua festa? *How many came to your party?*

5.18 Demonstrative Pronouns (Pronomi Dimostrativi)

5.19 (this, that) questo, quello, ...

	Singular	Plural	
Masculine	**questo** **quello**	**questi** **quelli**	this; these that; those
Feminine	**questa** **quella**	**queste** **quelle**	

e.g. Preferisco questa spiaggia perché **quella** è troppo affollata.
I prefer this beach because that one is too crowded.
Queste maglie sono di cotone e **quelle** sono di lana. *These vests are cotton and those are woollen.*
Questi occhiali sono molto più cari di **quelli**. *These spectacles are much dearer than those.*
Questo è un ottimo ristorante. *This is an excellent restaurant.*

- *The most used demonstrative pronouns have a form similar to that of demonstrative adjectives with the exception of* ***quelli*** *(see 3.7).*
- *Remember that pronouns substitute a noun , while adjectives accompany a noun.*

5.20 **Questi** (this man; the latter), **quegli** (that man; the former) are only used:
- in the masculine singular;
- as subject:
  Siamo andati al mare con Louis e John: **quegli** è francese, **questi** è inglese.
  We went to the seaside with Louis and John: the former is French, the latter is English.

5.21 **Costui** (this man; he; him;), **costei** (this woman; she; her;), **colui** (that man...), **colei** (that woman...); **costoro** (these people; they; them); **coloro** (those people; they; them) can be used:
- in a disparaging manner;
- as subject or object:
  Chi è **costui**? *Who's this man?*
  Non voglio più vedere **costei**. *I don't want to see this woman any more.*
  Costui è un disonesto. *This man is a rogue.*

- *The demonstrative pronouns* ***questi, quegli, costui, costei, costoro, colui, colei*** *and* ***coloro*** *are generally formal and seldom used.*

5.22 Indefinite Pronouns (Pronomi Indefiniti)

5.23 (one, someone, ...) uno, qualcuno, ...

	Singular	
Masculine	**uno**	one, someone
	qualcuno	somebody, someone, anybody, anyone
	ognuno	everybody, everyone
	chiunque	anybody, anyone
	qualcosa/qualche cosa	something, anything
	niente/nulla	nothing, anything
Feminine	**una**	
	qualcuna	
	ognuna	
	chiunque	
	-	
	-	

e.g. C'è **uno** che ti cerca. *Someone is looking for you.*
Ha telefonato **qualcuno**? *Has anyone 'phoned?*
Ognuno ha ricevuto un regalo. *Everyone received a present.*
Può entrare **chiunque**. *Anyone can come in.*
C'è **qualcosa** che non funziona. *There's something that doesn't work.*
Non è **niente,** non ti preoccupare. *It's nothing, don't worry.*
Vi serve **nulla**? *Do you need anything?*

5.24 (everyone, nobody, ...) ciascuno, nessuno, ...

Other indefinite pronouns are similar, in both form and use, to indefinite adjectives (see 3.12, 3.13, 3.14). Among these are:

- **ciascuno**, ciascuna *(everyone, everybody, each, each one)*
  nessuno, nessuna *(nobody, no-one)*
- **altro**, altra, altri, altre *(another, others)*
  molto, molta, molte, molti *(a lot, many)*
  parecchio, parecchia, parecchi, parecchie *(quite a lot, several)*
  poco, poca, pochi, poche *(a little, not much, few)*
  tanto, tanta ,tanti, tante *(a lot, many)*
  troppo, troppa, troppi, troppe *(too much, too many)*
  tutto, tutta, tutti, tutte *(all, everything, everybody)*
- **alcuno**, alcuna, alcuni, alcune *(anybody, anyone, some, a few)*

e.g. **Ciascuno** deve fare i compiti. *Everyone has to do his homework.*
Nessuna è più simpatica di Piera. *No one is nicer than Piera.*
Qualcuno ha fatto il bagno, **altri** hanno preso il sole. *Some had a swim, others sunbathed.*
Ha molti dischi, **alcuni** sono di musica classica. *He's got a lot of records, some are classical music.*
Vuoi **altro**? *Do you want anything else?*

5.25 POSSESSIVE PRONOUNS (PRONOMI POSSESSIVI)

MASCULINE SINGULAR		MASCULINE PLURAL		FEMININE SINGULAR		FEMININE PLURAL		
	mio		miei		mia		mie	(mine)
	tuo		tuoi		tua		tue	(yours) 'informal'
	Suo		Suoi		Sua		Sue	(yours) 'formal'
(il)	suo	(i)	suoi	(la)	sua	(le)	sue	(his, hers)
	nostro		nostri		nostra		nostre	(ours)
	vostro		vostri		vostra		vostre	(yours)
	loro		loro		loro		loro	(theirs)

e.g. Non trovo la mia penna, mi presti la **tua**? *I can't find my pen, will you lend me yours?*
Suo padre è inglese, **il mio** è italiano. *His father is English, mine is Italian.*

- *Possessive adjectives and pronouns have identical forms (see 3.8)*
- *Possessive pronouns agree with the implied object.*
- *Possessive pronouns are almost always preceded by the article.*
- ***I miei** and **i tuoi** can also indicate "my/your parents" or more generally "my/your family":*
  Vado in Italia con i miei. (I'm going to Italy with my family.)
- *To make a toast one can also say "**alla** + the possessive feminine singular":*
  Alla nostra (salute) [To our health!]. Alla tua! (To your health!)
- *Possessive pronouns in the feminine singular are often used in commercial and, less frequently, private correspondence:*
  Con riferimento alla Vostra del 24... (Referring to your letter of 24th...)
  Oggi ho ricevuto la tua... (Today I received your letter...)
- *The most common abbreviations of possessive adjectives and pronouns in commercial correspondence are:*
  s., S., (suo, Suo - your); V. (vostro, vostra - your); Vs. (Vostra lettera - your letter); ns. (nostro -our).

6. Common Uses of Si - Ci - Vi - Ne

6.1 Si

Reflexive

- **Si** (himself, herself, itself, themselves, oneself): Si lavano. *They wash themselves.*
- **Si** (his, her, their): Si lava le mani. *He washes his hands.*
- **Si** (each other; one another):
  Si scrivono una volta al mese. *They write to each other once a month.*

Impersonal

- Si (one; you; we; they; people) + 'verb' in the third person singular:
  Si dice che sia molto ambizioso. *People say he's very ambitious.*

Passive

- **Si** + 'verb' in the third person singular and plural:
  Si vende il vino novello. *The new wine is on sale.*
  Non si fanno sconti. *No discounts given.*

- *The reflexive unstressed pronoun **si** (= **sé** stressed) is used in the third person singular and plural. **Sé** can be emphasized by **stesso -a -i -e:** Pensano solo a sé stessi. (They think only of themselves.)*
- ***Si** changes to **se** when it is followed by **lo, la, li, le** or **ne.***
- ***Si** can take an apostrophe in front of a vowel: S'è fatto male. (He hurt himself.)*
- ***Sì** = yes.*
- ***Se** (conjunction) = if, whether.*

6.2 Ci and Vi

Personal Pronouns

- **Ci** (=noi) , **vi** (=voi): Ci invita. Vi saluta. *He invites us. He greets you.*
- **Ci** (=a noi), **vi** (=a voi): Ci presta il libro. Vi scrive. *He lends the book to us. He writes to you.*

Demonstrative Pronoun

- **Ci** = a ciò, di ciò, in ciò, su ciò, da ciò. (to it/this/that/, about it, ...):
  Pensaci! *Think about it!*
  Non ci fare caso. *Don't bother.*

Adverbs of Place

- **Ci/vi** = qua, là (here, there):
  Ci (=qua) venite tutti gli anni? *Do you come here every year?*
  Vi (=qua) resteremo due settimane. *We'll stay here two weeks.*
  C'è; c'era; ci sono, ... *There is; there was; there are, ...*

- ***Ci** and **vi** take an apostrophe only in front of the vowels **e** and, less frequently, **i:** C'è la doccia. C'indica la strada. (There is a shower. He shows us the way.)*
- ***Vi**, as an adverb of place, is seldom used in colloquial Italian.*

6.3 Ne

Pronoun

- **Ne** (of him/her/them): Non ne (=di lui) parli mai. *You never talk about him.*
  Ne (=di loro) parla sempre male. *He always talks badly of them.*
- **Ne** (by him/her/them): Ne (=da lui) rimase impressionato. *He was impressed by him.*
- **Ne** (of this/that...): Quanto ne (=di questo) vuoi? *How much do you want (of this)?*
  Ne abbiamo due. *We have two (of these).* Che cosa ne pensate? *What do you think (of this/that)?*

Adverb

- **Ne** (from here/there): Me ne vado. Ne uscì subito. *I'm going from here. He went out immediately.*

- ***Ne** can take an apostrophe: Non se n'era accorto. (He hadn't realized.) Me n'andai via. (I left.)*
- ***Né** ... **né** = neither... nor; either... or.*

7. The Verb: Moods and Tenses

Moods	Simple Tenses	e.g.		Compound Tenses	e.g	
INDICATIVE	present	**abito**	*I live, I am living, I do live*	perfect	**ho abitato**	*I have lived*
	imperfect	**abitavo**	*I was living, I used to live, I lived*	pluperfect	**avevo abitato**	*I had lived*
	past historic	**abitai**	*I lived*	past anterior	**ebbi abitato**	*I had lived*
	future	**abiterò**	*I' ll live, I am going to live*	future perfect	**avrò abitato**	*I'll have lived*
SUBJUNCTIVE	present	**abiti**	*I live*	perfect	**abbia abitato**	*I have lived*
	imperfect	**abitassi**	*I lived*	pluperfect	**avessi abitato**	*I had lived*
CONDITIONAL	present	**abiterei**	*I'd live*	perfect	**avrei abitato**	*I'd have lived*
IMPERATIVE	present	**abita!**	*live!*			
PARTICIPLE	present	**abitante**	*living*			
	past	**abitato**	*lived*			
GERUND	present	**abitando**	*living*	past	**avendo abitato**	*having lived*
INFINITIVE	present	**abitare**	*to live*	perfect	**avere abitato**	*to have lived*

☞ Italian verbs are divided into three groups according to the ending of the infinitive:

verbs ending in ***-are*** *(abitare, parlare, guardare, ...)*
verbs ending in ***-ere*** *(ripetere, vivere, leggere, ...)*
verbs ending in ***-ire*** *(partire, aprire, preferire, ...)*

Note

The English equivalents of the Italian verb tenses set out above are only given as simple examples since, in some cases, an Italian tense corresponds to a different one in English. For full explanations of tense translation refer to the relevant grammar sheet.

7.1 Present Indicative (Presente Indicativo)

	Essere *to be*	Avere *to have*	Abitare *to live*	Ripetere *to repeat*	Partire *to leave*
I	sono	ho	abit**o**	ripet**o**	part**o**
you	sei	hai	abit**i**	ripet**i**	part**i**
he, she, it	è	ha	abit**a**	ripet**e**	part**e**
we	siamo	abbiamo	abit**iamo**	ripet**iamo**	part**iamo**
you	siete	avete	abit**ate**	ripet**ete**	part**ite**
they	sono	hanno	abit**ano**	ripet**ono**	part**ono**

☞ The present tense is used:
- when the action takes place at the time the subject speaks:
  Compro il giornale. *I'm buying the newspaper.*
- to render an action that is habitual:
  Il telegiornale **inizia** alle 20.30. *The news starts at 20:30.*
- often in proverbs:
  Chi **cerca trova**. *Seek and you will find.*
- instead of the past tense to make a narrative more vivid:
  C. Colombo **parte** da Palos nel 1492 ... *In 1492 C. Columbus sailed from Palos ...*

Irregular Verbs

☞ • Many verbs of the third conjugation (**-IRE**) insert **-isc-** between the stem and the ending in the singular and in the third person plural.
Some of the most common are: capire (to understand); finire (to finish); preferire (to prefer); spedire (to send); suggerire (to suggest); ubbidire (to obey).

e.g.

Capire	Finire
cap-isc-o	fin-isc-o
cap-isc-i	fin-isc-i
cap-isc-e	fin-isc-e
capiamo	finiamo
capite	finite
cap-isc-ono	fin-isc-ono

☞
- Verbs ending in **-ciare** and **-giare** lose the **i** in front of an **i** .
- Verbs ending in **-care** and **-gare** take an **h** in front of an **i**.

e.g.

Pronunciare *to pronounce*	Viaggiare *to travel*	Cercare *to look for*	Pagare *to pay*
pronuncio	viaggio	cerco	pago
pronunc**i**	viagg**i**	cerc**hi**	pag**hi**
pronuncia	viaggia	cerca	paga
pronunciamo	viaggiamo	cerc**hi**amo	pag**h**iamo
pronunciate	viaggiate	cercate	pagate
pronunciano	viaggiano	cercano	pagano

Continued ➡

PRESENT Continued

Common Irregular Verbs

☞	ANDARE	*to go*	vado, vai, va; andiamo, andate, vanno.
	BERE	*to drink*	bevo, bevi, beve; beviamo, bevete, bevono.
	DARE	*to give*	do, dai, dà; diamo, date, danno.
	DIRE	*to say, to tell*	dico, dici, dice; diciamo, dite, dicono.
	FARE	*to make, to do*	faccio, fai, fa; facciamo, fate, fanno.
	PIACERE	*to like*	piaccio, piaci, piace; piacciamo, piacete, piacciono.
	RIMANERE	*to remain*	rimango, rimani, rimane; rimaniamo, rimanete, rimangono.
	SALIRE	*to go up*	salgo, sali, sale; saliamo, salite, salgono.
	SAPERE	*to know*	so, sai, sa; sappiamo, sapete, sanno.
	SCEGLIERE	*to choose*	scelgo, scegli, sceglie; scegliamo, scegliete, scelgono.
	STARE	*to stay*	sto, stai, sta; stiamo, state, stanno.
	TRADURRE	*to translate*	traduco, traduci, traduce; traduciamo, traducete, traducono.
	USCIRE	*to go out*	esco, esci, esce; usciamo, uscite, escono.
	VENIRE	*to come*	vengo, vieni, viene; veniamo, venite, vengono.
	DOVERE	*to have to*	devo, devi, deve; dobbiamo, dovete, devono.
	POTERE	*to be able*	posso, puoi, può; possiamo, potete, possono.
	VOLERE	*to want*	voglio, vuoi, vuole; vogliamo, volete, vogliono.

7.2. IMPERFECT INDICATIVE (IMPERFETTO INDICATIVO)

	ESSERE	AVERE	ABITARE	RIPETERE	PARTIRE
I	ero	avevo	abit**avo**	ripet**evo**	part**ivo**
you	eri	avevi	abit**avi**	ripet**evi**	part**ivi**
he,she,it	era	aveva	abit**ava**	ripet**eva**	part**iva**
we	eravamo	avevamo	abit**avamo**	ripet**evamo**	part**ivamo**
you	eravate	avevate	abit**avate**	ripet**evate**	part**ivate**
they	erano	avevano	abit**avano**	ripet**evano**	part**ivano**

☞ The imperfect is used to express:

- indeterminate duration of an action in the past:
  Alle dieci **studiavo** ancora. *At ten o'clock I was still studying.*
- continuity and repetition of an action in the past:
  Tutte le sere **guardavo** la televisione. *Every evening I used to watch TV.*
- two contemporaneous actions in the past:
  Mentre **scrivevo**, lui **ascoltava** la musica. *While I was writing, he was listening to music.*

Common Irregular Verbs

BERE	*to drink*	bevevo, bevevi, beveva; bevevamo, bevevate, bevevano.
DIRE	*to say, to tell*	dicevo, dicevi, diceva; dicevamo, dicevate, dicevano.
FARE	*to make, to do*	facevo, facevi, faceva; facevamo, facevate, facevano.
TRADURRE	*to translate*	traducevo, traducevi, traduceva; traducevamo, traducevate, traducevano.

7.3 PLUPERFECT (TRAPASSATO PROSSIMO)

ESSERE	AVERE	ABITARE	RIPETERE	PARTIRE
ero stato/a	avevo avuto	avevo abit**ato**	avevo ripet**uto**	ero part**ito**/a
eri stato/a	avevi avuto	avevi abitato	avevi ripetuto	eri partito/a
era stato/a	aveva avuto	aveva abitato	aveva ripetuto	era partito/a
eravamo stati/e	avevamo avuto	avevamo abitato	avevamo ripetuto	eravamo partiti/e
eravate stati/e	avevate avuto	avevate abitato	avevate ripetuto	eravate partiti/e
erano stati/e	avevano avuto	avevano abitato	avevano ripetuto	erano partiti/e

☞ The pluperfect is used to express:

- a past action that happened before another action, also in the past:
  Era appena uscito, quando telefonò Enrica. *He had just gone out, when Enrica 'phoned.*

☞ The pluperfect is formed:

- from the imperfect of **avere** or **essere** followed by the past participle of the verb (see 7.5).

7.4 Perfect Indicative (Passato Prossimo)

Essere	Avere	Abitare	Ripetere	Partire
sono stato/a	ho avuto	ho abit**ato**	ho ripet**uto**	sono part**ito/a**
sei stato/a	hai avuto	hai abitato	hai ripetuto	sei partito/a
è stato/a	ha avuto	ha abitato	ha ripetuto	è partito/a
siamo stati/e	abbiamo avuto	abbiamo abitato	abbiamo ripetuto	siamo partiti/e
siete stati/e	avete avuto	avete abitato	avete ripetuto	siete partiti/e
sono stati/e	hanno avuto	hanno abitato	hanno ripetuto	sono partiti/e

☞ It is used to indicate:
- an action that happened in a past that has not yet completely ended or has just ended: Quest'anno sono andato in Italia. *This year I've been to Italy.*
- an action in the past the effects of which are still continuing: C. Colombo ha scoperto l'America. *C. Columbus discovered America.*

☞ The perfect is formed from the present of **avere** or **essere** and the past participle of the verb.

☞ The past participle agrees with the subject when it is preceded by the auxiliary **essere:**
Maria è partita. Giorgio è partito. Maria e Rosa sono partite.
Maria has left. Giorgio has left. Maria and Rosa have left.
Giorgio e Antonio sono partiti. Maria e Giorgio sono partiti.
Giorgio and Antonio have left. Maria and Giorgio have left.

☞ The most common verbs that take the auxiliary **essere** are:
partire, arrivare, andare, venire, tornare, entrare, uscire, salire, scendere, stare, rimanere, piacere, riuscire, diventare.

7.5 Past Participle (Participio Passato)

Essere	Avere	Abitare	Ripetere	Partire
stato/a/i/e	avuto	abit**ATO**	ripet**UTO**	part**ITO**

Common Irregular Verbs

ACCENDERE *to turn on*	acceso	DIRE *to tell, to say*	detto
CHIUDERE *to close*	chiuso	FARE *to make, to do*	fatto
CORRERE *to run*	corso	LEGGERE *to read*	letto
DECIDERE *to decide*	deciso	SCRIVERE *to write*	scritto
METTERE *to put*	messo		
PRENDERE *to take*	preso	APRIRE *to open*	aperto
PROMETTERE *to promise*	promesso	OFFRIRE *to offer*	offerto
TRASCORRERE *to spend*	trascorso	SCEGLIERE *to choose*	scelto
		SPEGNERE *to turn off*	spento
CHIEDERE *to ask*	chiesto		
RISPONDERE *to reply*	risposto	BERE *to drink*	bevuto

ESSERE *to be*	stato/a/i/e
NASCERE *to be born*	nato/a/i/e
RIMANERE *to remain*	rimasto/a/i/e
VENIRE *to come*	venuto/a/i/e
SCENDERE *to come down*	sceso/a/i/e

7.6 Future (Futuro)

ESSERE	AVERE	ABITARE	RIPETERE	PARTIRE
sarò	avrò	abit**erò**	ripet**erò**	part**irò**
sarai	avrai	abit**erai**	ripet**erai**	part**irai**
sarà	avrà	abit**erà**	ripet**erà**	part**irà**
saremo	avremo	abit**eremo**	ripet**eremo**	part**iremo**
sarete	avrete	abit**erete**	ripet**erete**	part**irete**
saranno	avranno	abit**eranno**	ripet**eranno**	part**iranno**

☞ The future is used to indicate:

- an action that is still to come, with respect to the time in which one is talking:
  Domani **partirò** per l'Italia. *Tomorrow I'm leaving for Italy.*
- a doubt, a hypothesis:
  Avrà quindici anni. *He may be fifteen.*
- an order, referring to the future:
  Resterai a casa con tua sorella! *You'll stay at home with your sister!*

The present indicative is often used in spoken language to indicate an action that is still to happen: Domani parto per l'Italia. *Tomorrow I'm leaving for Italy.*

Common Irregular Verbs

☞ Verbs ending in **-ciare** and **-giare** lose the **i** in front of an **e**.

e.g.	**COMINCIARE**	*to start*	comincerò, comincerai, comincerà; cominceremo, comincerete, cominceranno.
	VIAGGIARE	*to travel*	viaggerò, viaggerai, viaggerà; viaggeremo, viaggerete, viaggeranno.

☞ Verbs ending in **-care** and **-gare** take an **h** in front of an **e**.

e.g.	**CERCARE**	*to look for*	cercherò, cercherai, cercherà; cercheremo, cercherete, cercheranno.
	PAGARE	*to pay*	pagherò, pagherai, pagherà; pagheremo, pagherete, pagheranno.
☞	**ANDARE**	*to go*	andrò, andrai, andrà; andremo, andrete, andranno.
	DOVERE	*to have to*	dovrò, dovrai, dovrà; dovremo, dovrete, dovranno.
	POTERE	*to be able*	potrò, potrai, potrà; potremo, potrete, potranno.
	SAPERE	*to know*	saprò, saprai, saprà; sapremo, saprete, sapranno.
	VEDERE	*to see*	vedrò, vedrai, vedrà; vedremo, vedrete, vedranno.
	VIVERE	*to live*	vivrò, vivrai, vivrà; vivremo, vivrete, vivranno.
☞	**BERE**	*to drink*	berrò, berrai, berrà; berremo, berrete, berranno.
	RIMANERE	*to remain*	rimarrò, rimarrai, rimarrà; rimarremo, rimarrete, rimarranno.
	TRADURRE	*to translate*	tradurrò, tradurrai, tradurrà; tradurremo, tradurrete, tradurranno.
	VENIRE	*to come*	verrò, verrai, verrà; verremo, verrete, verranno.
	VOLERE	*to want*	vorrò, vorrai, vorrà; vorremo, vorrete, vorranno.
☞	**DIRE**	*to say*	dirò, dirai, dirà; diremo, direte, diranno.
	FARE	*to make*	farò, farai, farà; faremo, farete, faranno.
	STARE	*to stay*	starò, starai, starà; staremo, starete, staranno.

7.7 FUTURE PERFECT (FUTURO ANTERIORE)

ESSERE	AVERE	ABITARE	RIPETERE	PARTIRE
sarò stato/a	avrò avuto	avrò abitato	avrò ripetuto	sarò partito/a
sarai stato/a	avrai avuto	avrai abitato	avrai ripetuto	sarai partito/a
sarà stato/a	avrà avuto	avrà abitato	avrà ripetuto	sarà partito/a
saremo stati/e	avremo avuto	avremo abitato	avremo ripetuto	saremo partiti/e
sarete stati/e	avrete avuto	avrete abitato	avrete ripetuto	sarete partiti/e
saranno stati/e	avranno avuto	avranno abitato	avranno ripetuto	saranno partiti/e

☞ The future perfect is normally used to indicate an action that will take place in the future but before another action also in the future:
Dopo che avrai mangiato, telefonerai a Renata. *After you've eaten, you'll 'phone Renata.*
Quando avrò finito i compiti, andrò al cinema. *When I have finished my homework, I'll go to the cinema.*

☞ The future perfect is formed from the simple future of **avere** or **essere** and the past participle of the verb.

7.8 PAST HISTORIC (PASSATO REMOTO)

ESSERE	AVERE	ABITARE	RIPETERE	PARTIRE
fui	ebbi	abit**ai**	ripet**ei**	part**ii**
fosti	avesti	abit**asti**	ripet**esti**	part**isti**
fu	ebbe	abit**ò**	ripet**é**	part**ì**
fummo	avemmo	abit**ammo**	ripet**emmo**	part**immo**
foste	aveste	abit**aste**	ripet**este**	part**iste**
furono	ebbero	abit**arono**	ripet**erono**	part**irono**

☞ The past historic is used to indicate an action that happened in the past and which has completely ended, having no relation with the present:
Due anni fa andarono a Venezia. *Two years ago they went to Venice.*
L'anno scorso Nicola comprò una Ferrari. *Last year Nicola bought a Ferrari.*

- *Verbs in - **ere** can have the following forms in the first and third person singular and the third person plural respectively: **-ei/-etti,-é/-ette,-erono/-ettero:***
  Crederono di avere ragione = Credettero di avere ragione. (They thought they were right.)
- *The past historic is used mainly in written language. In spoken language it is more often replaced by the perfect indicative, especially in Northern Italy:*
  L'anno scorso sono andata a Milano. (Last year I went to Milan.)

Common Irregular Verbs

BERE	*to drink*	bevvi, bevesti, bevve; bevemmo, beveste, bevvero.
CHIEDERE	*to ask*	chiesi, chiedesti, chiese; chiedemmo, chiedeste, chiesero.
CHIUDERE	*to close*	chiusi, chiudesti, chiuse; chiudemmo, chiudeste, chiusero.
CONOSCERE	*to know*	conobbi, conoscesti, conobbe; conoscemmo, conosceste, conobbero.
DARE	*to give*	diedi/detti, desti, diede/dette; demmo, deste , diedero/dettero.
DECIDERE	*to decide*	decisi, decidesti, decise; decidemmo, decideste, decisero.
DIRE	*to say, to tell*	dissi, dicesti, disse; dicemmo, diceste, dissero.
FARE	*to make, to do*	feci, facesti, fece; facemmo, faceste, fecero
LEGGERE	*to read*	lessi, leggesti, lesse; leggemmo, leggeste, lessero.
METTERE	*to put*	misi, mettesti, mise; mettemmo, metteste, misero.
NASCERE	*to be born*	nacqui, nascesti, nacque; nascemmo, nasceste, nacquero.
PERDERE	*to lose*	persi, perdesti, perse; perdemmo, perdeste, persero.
RIDERE	*to laugh*	risi, ridesti, rise; ridemmo, rideste, risero.
RIMANERE	*to remain*	rimasi, rimanesti, rimase; rimanemmo, rimaneste, rimasero.
RISPONDERE	*to reply*	risposi, rispondesti, rispose; rispondemmo, rispondeste, risposero.
SAPERE	*to know*	seppi, sapesti, seppe; sapemmo, sapeste, seppero.
SCEGLIERE	*to choose*	scelsi, scegliesti, scelse; scegliemmo, sceglieste, scelsero.
SCRIVERE	*to write*	scrissi, scrivesti, scrisse; scrivemmo, scriveste, scrissero.
STARE	*to stay*	stetti, stesti, stette; stemmo, steste, stettero.
TRADURRE	*to translate*	tradussi, traducesti ,tradusse; traducemmo, traduceste, tradussero.
VEDERE	*to see*	vidi,vedesti,vide; vedemmo, vedeste, videro.
VENIRE	*to come*	venni, venisti, venne; venimmo, veniste, vennero.
VINCERE	*to win*	vinsi, vincesti, vinse; vincemmo, vinceste, vinsero.
VIVERE	*to live*	vissi, vivesti, visse; vivemmo, viveste, vissero.
VOLERE	*to want*	volli, volesti, volle; volemmo, voleste, vollero.

- *Verbs in **-ere** are almost all irregular in the first and the third person singular and the third person plural.*

7.9 PRESENT CONDITIONAL (CONDIZIONALE PRESENTE)

ESSERE	AVERE	ABITARE	RIPETERE	PARTIRE
sarei	avrei	abit**erei**	ripet**erei**	part**irei**
saresti	avresti	abit**eresti**	ripet**eresti**	part**iresti**
sarebbe	avrebbe	abit**erebbe**	ripet**erebbe**	part**irebbe**
saremmo	avremmo	abit**eremmo**	ripet**eremmo**	part**iremmo**
sareste	avreste	abit**ereste**	ripet**ereste**	part**ireste**
sarebbero	avrebbero	abit**erebbero**	ripet**erebbero**	part**irebbero**

☞ The present conditional is normally used:
- to indicate a possibility that will take place under certain conditions:
  Comprerei la frutta (se fosse fresca). *I would buy the fruit (if it were fresh).*
- in polite forms of address.
  Vorrei un biglietto di andata e ritorno per Pisa. *I'd like a return ticket to Pisa.*

☞ For the irregular forms see the future tense.
e.g. **Comincerei, andrei, dovrei, saprei, potrei, vedrei, vivrei, berrei,** etc.

7.10 PERFECT CONDITIONAL (CONDIZIONALE PASSATO)

ESSERE	AVERE	ABITARE	RIPETERE	PARTIRE
sarei stato/a	avrei avuto	avrei abit**ato**	avrei ripet**uto**	sarei part**ito/a**
saresti stato/a	avresti avuto	avresti abitato	avresti ripetuto	saresti partito/a
sarebbe stato/a	avrebbe avuto	avrebbe abitato	avrebbe ripetuto	sarebbe partito/a
saremmo stati/e	avremmo avuto	avremmo abitato	avremmo ripetuto	saremmo partiti/e
sareste stati/e	avreste avuto	avreste abitato	avreste ripetuto	sareste partiti/e
sarebbero stati/e	avrebbero avuto	avrebbero abitato	avrebbero ripetuto	sarebbero partiti/e

☞ The perfect conditional is normally used:
- to indicate a possibility that could have happened in the past under certain conditions:
  Avrei comprato la frutta (se fosse stata fresca). *I would have bought the fruit (if it had been fresh).*
- to express an action happening after another in the past:
  Hanno detto che **sarebbero andati** a Parigi. *They said they would go to Paris.*

☞ The perfect conditional is formed from the present conditional of **avere** or **essere** and the past participle of the verb.

7.11 PRESENT SUBJUNCTIVE (CONGIUNTIVO PRESENTE)

ESSERE	AVERE	ABITARE	RIPETERE	PARTIRE
sia	abbia	abiti	ripeta	parta
sia	abbia	abiti	ripeta	parta
sia	abbia	abiti	ripeta	parta
siamo	abbiamo	abit**iamo**	ripet**iamo**	part**iamo**
siate	abbiate	abit**iate**	ripet**iate**	part**iate**
siano	abbiano	abit**ino**	ripet**ano**	part**ano**

The subjunctive usually depends on another verb that indicates opinion, possibility, uncertainty, desire, ... [**credere** (to believe/think); **pensare** (to think/suppose); **sperare** (to hope), ...]

e.g. Penso che loro **abbiano** ragione. *I think they are right.*
Speriamo che il treno **sia** in orario. *Let's hope the train will be on time.*

In secondary clauses the subjunctive is always used after:
a condizione che (on condition that); affinché (so that); a meno che (unless); benché (although); nel caso che (in case); prima che (before). Bisogna che (it is necessary that); è meglio che (it is better that); è un peccato che (it is a pity that), ...

e.g. Telefonagli prima che **esca**. *'Phone him before he goes out.*
È un peccato che tu non **sia** qui con noi. *It's a pity you're not here with us.*

In spoken language the subjunctive is often replaced by the indicative.

Common Irregular Verbs

ANDARE	*to go*	vada, vada, vada; andiamo, andiate, vadano.
BERE	*to drink*	beva, beva, beva; beviamo, beviate, bevano.
DARE	*to give*	dia, dia, dia; diamo, diate, diano.
DIRE	*to say, to tell*	dica, dica, dica; diciamo, diciate, dicano.
DOVERE	*to have to*	debba, debba, debba; dobbiamo, dobbiate, debbano.
FARE	*to make, to do*	faccia, faccia, faccia; facciamo, facciate, facciano.
POTERE	*to be able*	possa, possa, possa, possiamo, possiate, possano.
SCEGLIERE	*to choose*	scelga, scelga, scelga; scegliamo, scegliate, scelgano.
STARE	*to stay*	stia, stia, stia; stiamo, stiate, stiano.
TENERE	*to keep*	tenga, tenga, tenga; teniamo, teniate, tengano.
TRADURRE	*to translate*	traduca, traduca, traduca; traduciamo, traduciate, traducano.
USCIRE	*to go out*	esca, esca, esca; usciamo, usciate, escano.
VENIRE	*to come*	venga, venga, venga; veniamo, veniate, vengano.
VOLERE	*to want*	voglia, voglia, voglia; vogliamo, vogliate, vogliano.

7.12 IMPERATIVE (IMPERATIVO)

	ESSERE	AVERE	GIRARE	PRENDERE	PARTIRE
(tu)	sii	abbi	gir**a**	prend**i**	part**i**
(Lei)	sia	abbia	gir**i**	prend**a**	part**a**
(noi)	siamo	abbiamo	gir**iamo**	prend**iamo**	part**iamo**
(voi)	siate	abbiate	gir**ate**	prend**ete**	part**ite**
(Loro)	siano	abbiano	gir**ino**	prend**ano**	part**ano**

☞ The imperative expresses a direct or indirect order, but also an exhortation, advice or a prayer.
Vieni subito qui! *Come here immediately!* **Giri** a destra! *Turn right!*
Non fate rumore ! *Don't make a noise!*
Studia, che domani ci sono gli esami! *Study, because you have exams tomorrow!*
Ascolta i consigli del medico: **mangia** meno dolci! *Listen to the doctor's advice: eat fewer sweets!*

- *The imperative does not have the first person singular* ***io.***
- *With* ***tu,noi*** *and* ***voi*** *we use the imperative.*
- *With* ***Lei*** *and* ***Loro*** *we use the indirect imperative (=present subjunctive), which turns the order into an invitation.*
- *The future imperative = the future indicative: Verrai al mare! (You will come to the seaside!)*

Negative imperative

- The negative imperative = non + imperative: (voi) Non girate a destra! *Don't turn right!*
- The imperative negative with the second singular person **tu** = non + infinitive:
  (tu) Non girare a destra! *Don't turn right!*

Imperative and pronouns

The imperative with unstressed pronouns, **ci** or **ne**, is usually formed in the following ways:

- Imperative + pronouns (the verb and the pronouns form one word): Parlagli! Invitiamolo!
- Pronouns + indirect imperative (pronouns and verb are separate): Gli parli! Glielo scriva!

Negative imperative and pronouns.

- Non + imperative + pronouns: Non invitiamolo! Non scriveteglielo!
- Non + infinitive + pronouns (with the second person singular **tu**):
  Non parlargli! Non invitarlo!
- Non + pronouns + indirect imperative: Non gli parli! Non ce le spediscano!

Common Irregular Verbs

ANDARE *to go*	va', vada; andiamo, andate, vadano.
DARE *to give*	da', dia; diamo, date, diano.
DIRE *to say*	di', dica; diciamo, dite, dicano.
FARE *to make*	fa', faccia, facciamo, fate, facciano.
STARE *to stay*	sta', stia; stiamo, state, stiano.

- *Va' (=vai), da' (=dai), fa' (=fai), sta' (=stai)*
- *When* ***va', da', di', fa'*** *and* ***sta'*** *are followed by a personal pronoun (with the exception of* ***gli****), the consonant is doubled.*
  e.g. Valle a chiedere scusa! (Va' + le = valle). Dammi il mio libro! (Da' + mi = dammi).
  Fagli vedere le fotografie! (Fa' + gli = fagli).

7.13 Gerund (Gerundio)

	Essere	Avere	Abitare	Ripetere	Partire
Present	essendo	avendo	abit**ando**	ripet**endo**	part**endo**
Past	essendo stato/a/i/e	avendo avuto	avendo abitato	avendo ripetuto	essendo partito/a/i/e

☞
- The gerund is used to indicate an action that specifies or modifies the principal action:
  Andando a scuola, ho visto Enzo. *While I was going to school, I saw Enzo.*
  Avendo mangiato troppo, si sentì male. *Having eaten too much, he felt sick.*

- The gerund (particularly the past gerund) is rarely used and is normally replaced by explicit phrases:
  Mentre andavo a scuola, ho visto Enzo. *While I was going to school, I saw Enzo.*
  Poiché aveva mangiato troppo, si sentì male. *As he had eaten too much, he felt sick.*

- The past gerund is formed from the present gerund of the auxiliary **avere** or **essere** and the past participle of the verb.

- The present gerund is also used to indicate progressive action: **stare + gerund:**
  Sto studiando il gerundio. *I am studying the gerund.*
  Stavo partendo per l'Italia. *I was leaving for Italy.*

7.14 Infinitive (Infinito)

Present	ESSERE	AVERE	ABITARE	RIPETERE	PARTIRE
Perfect	essere stato/a/i/e	aver avuto	aver abitato	aver ripetuto	essere partito/a/i/e

☞ The infinitive usually depends on another verb or is used in secondary clauses:
Devo **scrivere** a Giovanna. *I have to write to Giovanna.*
Non è più andato in quel ristorante dopo **essere stato** male.
He didn't go to that restaurant any more after being ill.

☞ The infinitive can be used:
- to give an order:
  Rallentare. *Slow down.* Dare la precedenza *Give way.*
- to form the imperative with **tu**:
  Non urlare! *Don't shout!*
- to give instruction:
  Scrivere in stampatello. *Write in block letters.*
- as a noun:
  Nuotare è rilassante. *Swimming is relaxing.* Ballare è divertente. *Dancing is enjoyable.*

☞ The present infinitive can be used to indicate an action in preparation: **stare + per** + **infinitive**:
Sto per uscire. *I'm about to go out.* Stavo per partire. *I was going to leave.*

Preposition and the infinitive

☞ Some verbs are followed by the infinitive without a preposition. Among these verbs are:
potere (to be able), **dovere** (to have to), **volere** (to want):
Posso chiederti un favore? Can I ask you a favour?
Devo studiare. *I have to study.* Vorrei andare al cinema. *I'd like to go to the cinema.*

☞ **Common verbs with a preposition before the infinitive are:**

cominciare a	*to start*
continuare a	*to go on*
imparare a	*to learn*
insegnare a	*to teach*
decidere di	*to decide*
dimenticare di	*to forget*
cercare di	*to try*
promettere di	*to promise*
smettere di	*to stop*
sperare di	*to hope*

e.g. Ha cominciato a lavorare. *He started working.*
Ho dimenticato di spedire la cartolina. *I forgot to send the card.*

7.15 Reflexive Verbs (Verbi Riflessivi)

INDICATIVE

	PRESENT (I enjoy myself, ...)	PERFECT (I have enjoyed myself, ...)	
(Io)	**mi** diverto	mi sono divertito/a	myself
(tu)	**ti** diverti	ti sei divertito/a	yourself (informal)
(lui, lei ,Lei)	**si** diverte	si è divertito/a	himself, herself, yourself (formal)
(noi)	**ci** divertiamo	ci siamo divertiti/e	ourselves
(voi)	**vi** divertite	vi siete divertiti/e	yourselves
(loro)	**si** divertono	si sono divertiti/e	themselves

e.g. Mi lavo. *I wash myself.*
Ci siamo lavati. *We have washed ourselves.*
Si è bruciata. *She has burnt herself.*

☞ *The reflexive form is generally used when the subject of the verb is the same as the object.*
☞ *The pronouns **mi, ti, si, ci, vi** precede the verb.*
☞ *They follow the verb, joining with it in a single word, only in the following cases:*
- *with the imperative (**tu, noi**): Vestiti! (Get dressed!) Vestiamoci! (Let's get dressed!)*
- *with the past participle: Vestitosi, è uscito. (After getting dressed, he went out.)*
- *with the infinitive: Bisogna vestirsi. (We must get dressed.)*
- *with the gerund: Ha perso un bottone vestendosi. (He lost a button while getting dressed.)*

☞ *In compound tenses the auxiliary **essere** is always used.*

The most common reflexive verbs are:

ABBRONZARSI	*to get tanned*	INTERESSARSI A/DI	*to take an interest in*
ABITUARSI A	*to accustom oneself*	LAMENTARSI	*to complain*
ACCOMODARSI	*to come in; to sit down*	PERDERSI	*to get lost*
ALZARSI	*to get up; to stand up*	PETTINARSI	*to comb one's hair*
ANNOIARSI	*to be bored*	PREPARARSI	*to get ready*
ARRABBIARSI	*to get angry*	PREOCCUPARSI	*to worry*
AVVICINARSI A	*to approach*	ROMPERSI	*to break*
BRUCIARSI	*to burn oneself*	SBRIGARSI	*to be quick, to hurry up*
CHIAMARSI	*to be called*	SCUSARSI	*to apologize*
CONGRATULARSI CON	*to congratulate*	SENTIRSI	*to feel*
DIVERTIRSI	*to enjoy oneself*	SVEGLIARSI	*to wake up*
FERMARSI	*to stop*	VERGOGNARSI	*to be ashamed*
INCONTRARSI	*to meet*	VESTIRSI	*to get dressed*

8. Numerals (Numerali)

CARDINALS (1, 2, ...)	ORDINALS (first, second, ...)
1 uno,-a	primo, -a, -i, -e
2 due	secondo, ...
3 tre	terzo
4 quattro	quarto
5 cinque	quinto
6 sei	sesto
7 sette	settimo
8 otto	ottavo
9 nove	nono
10 dieci	decimo
11 undici	undicesimo
12 dodici	dodicesimo
13 tredici	tredicesimo
14 quattordici	quattordicesimo
15 quindici	quindicesimo
16 sedici	sedicesimo
17 diciassette	diciassettesimo
18 diciotto	diciottesimo
19 diciannove	diciannovesimo
20 venti	ventesimo
21 ventuno	ventunesimo
22 ventidue	ventiduesimo
23 ventitré	ventitreesimo
28 ventotto	ventottesimo
30 trenta	trentesimo
40 quaranta	quarantesimo
50 cinquanta	cinquantesimo
60 sessanta	sessantesimo
70 settanta	settantesimo
80 ottanta	ottantesimo
90 novanta	novantesimo
100 cento	centesimo
101 centouno	centunesimo
200 duecento	duecentesimo
400 quattrocento	quattrocentesimo
500 cinquecento	cinquecentesimo
900 novecento	novecentesimo
1.000 mille	millesimo

1.001 milleuno
1.002 milledue
1.003 milletré
1800 milleottocento
1975 millenovecentosettantacinque

1976 millenovecentosettantasei
1977 millenovecentosettantasette
1978 millenovecentosettantotto
1990 millenovecentonovanta
1991 millenovecentonovantuno

2.000 duemila
10.000 diecimila
100.000 centomila
1.000.000 un milione

Continued ➥

8.1 Cardinal Numbers

☞ Gender and plural.
- **Zero** takes the plural: due zeri, tre zeri, ...
- **Uno** takes the feminine and follows the rules of the indefinite article: uno studente, una studentessa, ...
- The plural of **mille** is -**mila** (1.000 = mille ; 2.000 = duemila; 400.000 = quattrocentomila).
- **Milione, bilione, miliardo,** etc. take the plural (milioni, bilioni, miliardi, etc.) and link to the noun that follows them by means of the preposition **di**: due milioni di abitanti, tre miliardi di lire, ...
- All other numbers are invariable: due studenti, due studentesse, ...

☞ **Tre** has an accent in compound numbers: ventitré, centotré, ...

☞ There is elision when **uno** and **otto** follow **venti, trenta, quaranta** , etc.: ventuno, trentotto, trentuno, trentotto, ...

☞ When **cento** and **mille** are followed by another number, they can also be written separated by **e**: 101 = cento e uno; 1.080 = mille e ottanta, ...

☞ In Italian a full stop is used when a comma is used in English and viceversa: 1.000=*1,000*

☞ Colloquially abbreviations are often used, particularly to indicate the hundreds above a thousand: tremila e due = tremila e duecento. Novemila e cinque = novemila e cinquecento.

☞ Arabic numerals are used in general:
- to avoid excessively long words: 24.546 lire (but in cheques, current accounts, etc. they are also written in one word: ventiquattromilacinquecentoquarantasei lire.)
- in dates: 2 maggio, 6 giugno, ... (with the exception of the first day of the month: 1° maggio, 1° giugno, ...)

☞ Common idiomatic phrases: in due parole (in a few words); è qui a due passi (is only just around the corner).

8.2 Ordinal Numbers

☞
- Ordinal numbers are variable: primo, prima, primi, prime, ...
- Apart from the first ten, they are formed by adding **-esimo** to the cardinal numbers without the last vowel: undicesimo, dodicesimo, ...
- They can be written in two ways: I, II, ... or 1°, 1ª , 2°, 2ª , ...

8.3 Fractions

☞
- 1/2 (un mezzo or una metà), 1/3 (un terzo), 1/4 (un quarto), 1/5 (un quinto), 1/6 (un sesto), 2/2 (due mezzi), 2/3 (due terzi), 3/4 (tre quarti), ...
- **Mezzo** agrees with the noun to which it refers (e.g .mezzo litro di vino, mezza bottiglia), but usually when it follows the noun it is invariable (e.g. è l'una e mezzo, sono le due e mezzo).

8.4 Multiple Numbers

- **Doppio** (double), **triplo** (triple), **quadruplo** (quadruple), **quintuplo** (quintuple), etc.

8.5 Collective Numbers

- **Paio** (pair; a couple), **coppia** (couple; pair), **decina** (ten; about ten), **dozzina** (dozen; about a dozen), ... **centinaio** (a hundred; about a hundred), **migliaio** (thousand; about a thousand) Plural: paia, coppie, decine, dozzine, ... centinaia, migliaia.
- **Entrambi** (both) takes the feminine: entrambi i ragazzi, entrambe le ragazze. **Ambedue** (both) is invariable: ambedue i ragazzi, ambedue le ragazze.

8.6 Iterative Numbers

- Una volta (once), due volte (twice), tre volte (three times), etc.

8.7 Mathematical Signs

- + (più), - (meno), x (**moltiplicato** per), : (**diviso** per), = (uguale a), % (per cento).

9. DATES AND TIME (LA DATA E L'ORA)

9.1 Calendar

Che data è oggi?	*What is the date today?*	È il due di novembre.	*It is the second of November.*
Quanti ne abbiamo?	*What day is it today?*	Ne abbiamo tre.	*It is the third.*
Che giorno è oggi?	*Which day of the week is it today?*	È lunedì.	*It is Monday.*

Giorni (Days): lunedì, martedì, mercoledì, giovedì, venerdì, sabato, domenica.
Monday, Tuesday, Wednesday, Thursday, Friday, Saturday, Sunday.

Mesi (Months):
gennaio, febbraio, marzo, aprile, maggio, giugno, luglio, agosto, settembre, ottobre,novembre, dicembre.
January, February, March, April, May, June, July, August, September, October, November, December.

Stagioni (Seasons): primavera, estate, autunno, inverno.
spring, summer, autumn, winter.

Note

☞
- *The ordinal number is used only for the first day of the month: è il primo (di) novembre.*
- *The names of the months and of the days of the week are nearly always written with a small letter.*

9.2 Clock

a che ora?	*at what time?*	ora	*hour*
alle nove	*at nine o'clock*	precise (alle due ...)	*at two o'clock sharp*
avanti di tre minuti	*three minutes fast*	preciso	*exact, precise*
che ora è/che ore sono?	*what time is it?*	quando?	*when?*
è l'una	*it is one o'clock*	quarto	*quarter*
indietro di sei minuti	*six minutes slow*	secondo	*second*
mezz'ora	*half an hour*	sono le due e cinque	*it's five past two*
mezzanotte	*midnight*	sono le due meno cinque	*it's five to two*
mezzo/mezza	*half*	sono le tre e mezzo	*it's half past three*
mezzogiorno	*midday*	sono le tre e un quarto	*it's a quarter past three*
minuto	*minute*	sono le tre	*it's three o'clock*

☞
- To tell the time in colloquial Italian only the cardinal numbers from 1 to 12 are normally used: Faccio colazione alle sette e venti (7.20). Di solito ceniamo alle sette e venti (19.20).
  I have breakfast at seven twenty . We usually have supper at seven twenty.
- The cardinal numbers from 1 to 24 are used for timetables of trains, airlines, etc.
  Il treno per Pisa parte alle venti e trenta (20.30). *The train to Pisa leaves at twenty thirty (20:30).*

9.3 Expressions of Time with 'Da' and 'Per'

da (for)	Abito a Londra **da** sei anni. (I've been living in London for six years.) Studio italiano **da** due anni. (I've been studying Italian for two years.)
da (since)	Non li vediamo **dalle** sette. (We haven't seen them since seven o'clock.)
da (as from,from)	**Da** oggi in poi. (From today onwards.)
per (for)	Ho studiato italiano **per** due anni. (I studied Italian for two years.)
per (by)	Sarà pronto **per** lunedì. (It will be ready by Monday.)

10. Prepositions (Preposizioni Semplici)

The most used prepositions are:

di, a, da, in, con, su, per, tra/fra

DI (of, by, from)
- Vorrei una scatola **di** cioccolatini. *I'd like a box of chocolates.*
- È un film **di** Fellini. *It's a film by Fellini.*
- **Di** dove sei? *Where are you from?*

A (to, at, in)
- Vado **a** Londra. *I'm going to London.*
- Resto **a** casa. *I'm staying at home.*
- Abito **a** Padova. *I live in Padua.*

DA (from, to, by, at)
- **Da** dove vieni? *Where do you come from?*
- Andiamo **da** Bruno? *Shall we go to Bruno's?*
- Sono conosciuti **da** tutti. *They are known by everyone.*
- Siamo stati tutta la mattina **da** Giovanna. *We've been at Giovanna's all morning.*

IN (in, to, at, by)
- È **in** giardino. *He's in the garden.*
- Vado **in** Australia. *I'm going to Australia.*
- Non è **in** casa. *He's not at home.*
- Verremo **in** treno. *We'll come by train.*

PER (for, through, to)
- Ho un regalo per te. *I have a present for you.*
- È passato per i campi. *He went through the fields.*
- Vorrei un biglietto **per** Pisa. *I'd like a ticket to Pisa.*

CON (with)
- È uscita **con** Elena. *She's gone out with Elena.*

SU (on)
- La borsa è **su** quella poltrona. *The bag is on that chair.*

TRA/ FRA (between, among, in)
- Arriverà tra l'una e le due. *He'll arrive between one and two.*
- **Tra** gli invitati, ci sono quattro americani. *There are four Americans among the guests.*
- Torno **fra** dieci minuti. *I'll be back in ten minutes.*

- *These prepositions have no meaning of their own and therefore cannot be translated literally; the translation given refers to the most common use.*
- ***Di** can take an apostrophe in front of a vowel: d'inverno, d'origine.*
- ***Da** takes an apostrophe only in front of a few expressions: d'altra parte, d'altronde, d'ora in poi.*
- ***A** can take **d** in front of a vowel for phonetical reasons: andiamo ad Alassio, ad esempio.*
- ***Tra=Fra** the choice only depends on phonetics: tra i fratelli, fra le traduzioni.*

10.1 PREPOSITIONS & DEFINITE ARTICLES (PREPOSIZIONI ARTICOLATE)

	+ il	lo	la	l'	i	gli	le
a	al	allo	alla	all'	ai	agli	alle
da	dal	dallo	dalla	dall'	dai	dagli	dalle
su	sul	sullo	sulla	sull'	sui	sugli	sulle
di	del	dello	della	dell'	dei	degli	delle
in	nel	nello	nella	nell'	nei	negli	nelle

e.g. Partirò **alle** sei. *I'll leave at six.*
Vada dritto fino **all'**incrocio. *Go straight on as far as the crossing.*
È andata **dalla** sua amica. *She's gone to her friend's.*
Bisogna salire **sul** terrazzo, *It's necessary to go up to the terrace.*
La camicia è nel cassetto. *The shirt is in the drawer.*
Verrà **con le** sue cugine, *She'll come with her cousins.*
Grazie **per l'**ospitalità! *Thank you for the hospitality!*

- *With the prepositions* ***con*** *and* ***per*** *the union with the article is optional but is now considered obsolete and in some cases can cause ambiguity of meaning (****collo, colla, pelle*** *also mean neck, glue, skin/leather).*
- ***Tra*** *and* ***fra*** *are never joined to the article: L'ho trovato* ***tra i*** *miei vestiti.*

11. Conjunctions (Congiunzioni)

Common conjunctions

Conjunctions joining two words in a single phrase or two separate phrases

E (and)	Ha i capelli corti **e** lisci. *Her hair is short and straight.*
(**ed** in front of a vowel)	Ha salutato tutti ed è uscito. *He said goodbye to everybody and went out.*
Anche (also; too)	C'erano **anche** i suoi genitori. *His parents were there too.*
O (or)	Arriveranno oggi **o** domani. *They will arrive today or tomorrow.*
Ma, però (but; however)	Lei è simpatica, **ma** suo fratello è troppo arrogante. *She is nice, but her brother is too arrogant.* Non potrò andare alla sua festa, **però** gli ho spedito un regalo. *I won't be able to go to his party, however I sent him a present.*
Infatti (in fact)	Sono già partiti, **infatti** le persiane sono chiuse. *They've already left, in fact the shutters are closed.*
Dunque, perciò (so; therefore)	L'autobus è appena passato, **perciò** dovremo andare a piedi. *The bus has just gone, so we'll have to walk.* **Dunque** faremo così! *Therefore we'll do this!*
Sia...sia (both ... and; whether ... or)	Abbiamo invitato **sia** i tuoi amici **sia** quelli di tuo fratello. *We've invited both your friends and your brother's.*
O... o (either ... or)	Sono andati **o** a ballare **o** al cinema. *They've either gone dancing or to the cinema.*
Non solo ... ma anche (not only ... but also)	È un film **non solo** noioso **ma anche** lungo. *It's a film that's not only boring but also long.*
Né ... né (neither...nor) (either...or)	Non vuole **né** pane **né** grissini. *He doesn't want either bread or bread sticks.*

Conjunctions joining two or more phrases, of which one is governed by the other

Che (that)	Spero **che** tu stia meglio. *I hope you are better.*
Se (if)	Non sappiamo se inviterà Giorgio. *We don't know if she'll invite Giorgio.*
Perché (because)	Non sono venuto **perché** non stavo bene. *I didn't come because I wasn't well.*
Poiché (as, since)	**Poiché** piove, restiamo a casa. *As it's raining, we'll stay at home.*
Come se (as if).	Fai **come se fossi** a casa tua. *Behave as if you were at home.*
Anche se (even if)	**Anche** se lavorassi tutta la notte, non riuscirei a finire. *Even if I worked all night, I wouldn't manage to finish.*
Se (if; whether; unless)	**Se** ci sarà il sole, andremo al mare. *If the sun is out, we'll go to the seaside.*
A condizione che (provided that)	Andranno al mare, **a condizione** che non piova. *They'll go to the seaside provided that it's not raining.*
Quando (when)	Uscirai **quando** avrai finito i compiti! *You'll go out when you've finished your homework!*
Mentre (while)	**Mentre** andavo a scuola, ho incontrato Claudio. *I met Claudio while I was going to school.*

12. ACCENTS (ACCENTI)

An accent is added:

- on words of two or more syllables when the stress falls on the vowel of the last syllable.
  e.g. Qualità, laggiù, università, perché, però, partì, andò, andrà, ventitré, lunedì, etc.

- on the following monosyllables: **può, già, più, ciò** and **giù.**

- on some monosyllables to distinguish them from other words with the same form but different meanings:

è verb (he/she/it is)	**e** conjunction (and)
dà verb (he/she/it gives)	**da** preposition (from,to, ...)
là adverb of place (there)	**la** article, pronoun (the; her)
lì adverb of place (there)	**li** pronoun (them)
né conjunction (nor, ...)	**ne** pronoun and adverb (of this, from here, ...)
sì affirmative (yes)	**si** pronoun, impersonal, passive (himself, one, ...)
sé pronoun (himself, ...)	**se** conjunction (if, whether)
tè noun (tea)	**te** pronoun (you)

e.g. Lui **è** italiano **e** loro sono inglesi. *He is Italian and they are English.*
Lui **dà** il libro a Pietro. Viene **da** Firenze. *He gives the book to Pietro. He comes from Florence.*
La penna è **là** sul tavolo. **La** vedi? *The pen is there on the table. Can you see it?*
I libri sono **lì** accanto alla penna. **Li** vedi? *The books are there close to the pen. Can you see them?*
Né lui **né** lei. **Ne vuoi** ancora? *Neither him nor her. Would you like some more of it?*
Pensa solo a **sé**. **Se** finirò i compiti, andrò al cinema. *He thinks only about himself. If I finish my homework, I will go to the cinema.*
Sì, sono americano. **Si** dice che sia americano. *Yes, I am American. He is said to be American.*
Hai comperato il **tè**? Beato **te**! *Did you buy the tea? Lucky you!*

- The others monosyllables are not accented.
  e.g. Va, fa, su, sto, sta, qui, qua, tra, fra, me, so, fu, no, etc.

☞ *The Italian accents on the last vowel are :*

- *acute on closed **é** : né, sé, perché, poiché, ripeté, ventitré.*
- grave on open **è** and , usually, on the other vowels (à, ù, ò and ì):
  è, caff**è**, per**ò**, perci**ò**, t**è**, gi**à**, pi**ù**, cos**ì**, etc.
- The difference between the two types of accents is diminishing and it is common to add a grave accent to all vowels when necessary.

☞ • **Sé** may be reinforced by the word s**tesso** and in this case is usually not accented. The use of an accent is nevertheless common and acceptable, particularly in places where the meaning may be ambiguous (**sé** stessi, sé stesse, without an accent could also mean "if I were, if she/he were")

☞ • Remember that:
- the preposition **a** and the verb **ha** are never accented:
- a silent **h** is added to distinguish **ho** (I have), **ha** (he/she/it has), **hai** (you have), **hanno** (they have), from **o** (or), **a** (to), **ai** (to the), and **anno** (year).

13. LANGUAGE FUNCTIONS (WHAT WE DO WITH THE LANGUAGE)

13.1 Greeting People

Ciao!	Hallo!, Hi.
Salve!	Hallo!
Buongiorno!	Good morning!/Good afternoon!
Buongiorno, signor/signora/signorina...	Good morning, Mr./Mrs/Miss
Buonasera...	Good evening ...

13.2 Introducing Someone And Being Introduced

Questo/questa è ...	This is ...
Le presento il signor...[formal]	This is Mr...
Posso presentarle il signor... [formal]	May I introduce Mr... to you?
Mi chiamo...	My name is ...
Ciao, (io sono Carla).	Hallo! (I am Carla).
Piacere!	How do you do?
Molto lieto! [formal]	How do you do?

13.3 Taking Leave

Ciao!	Bye!
(Ciao), a presto!	See you soon!
Arrivederci!	Goodbye!
ArrivederLa! [formal]	Goodbye!
Buonanotte!	Good night!
A più tardi!	See you later!
A domani!	See you tomorrow!

13.4 Attracting Attention

Scusa...	Excuse me....
(Mi) scusi... [formal]	Excuse me...
Senta, per favore... [formal]	Excuse me, please...

13.5 Congratulating

Bravo!	Well done!
Congratulazioni!	Congratulations!
Sei stato bravissimo!	You've done very well!

13.6 Expressing Good Wishes

Auguri!	Best wishes!
I migliori auguri!	All the best!
Ti auguro...	I wish you..
Le auguro...[formal]	I wish you..
Buon Natale!	Merry Christmas!
Buon Anno!	Happy New Year!
Buona Pasqua!	Happy Easter!
Buon compleanno!	Happy Birthday!
Buone vacanze!	Have a good holiday!
Buon viaggio!	Have a good trip!

13.7 Expressing And Responding To Thanks

Grazie!	Thanks!
Grazie mille!	Thanks a lot/ thank you very much!
Grazie per ...	Thank you for ...
Ti ringrazio!	Thank you!
La ringrazio. [formal]	Thank you!
Non so come ringraziarti!	I don't know how to thank you!
Non so come ringraziarLa! [formal]	I don't know how to thank you!
Prego!	Don't mention it!
Di niente!	It's all right!
È stato un piacere!	It has been a pleasure!

13.8 Expressing Lack Of Understanding

Come, (scusa)?	Pardon?
Scusi, come ha detto? [formal]	(I beg your) pardon?
Prego? (Non ho capito!)	(I beg your) pardon?
Non capisco.	I don't understand.
Non ho capito.	I haven't understood.
Vuole ripetere, prego? [formal]	Would you repeat it, please?
Che cosa vuol dire?	What does it mean?
Puoi ripetere, per favore?	Can you repeat it, please?
Non è chiaro.	It is not clear.
E cioè?	What do you mean?

13.9 Expressing Agreement And Disagreement

Sono d'accordo.	I agree.
Hai (proprio) ragione!	You're right!
Naturalmente!	Of course!
Giusto!	Right!
Non sono d'accordo!	I don't agree!
Sbagli!	You are wrong!
Non è vero!	It's not true!
Per niente!	Not at all!

Continued ➥

13.10 Expressing Surprise

Che sorpresa!	What a surprise!
Che bella sorpresa!	What a nice surprise!
Questa sì che è una sorpresa!	This is a real surprise!
Davvero!	No kidding?
Non ci credo!	I can't believe it!
No!	No!

13.11 Expressing Hope

Speriamo!	Let's hope so!
Speriamo di sì.	I hope so!
Magari!	If only!
Speriamo che tu stia meglio! [see 7.11 Subjunctive]	I hope you'll be better.

13.12 Expressing Satisfaction

Magnifico!	Wonderful!
Che bello!	How lovely!
Sono contento/soddisfatto ...	I'm very happy/satisfied ...
E proprio quello che desideravo.	It's just what I wanted.
È molto bello!	It's lovely!

13.13 Expressing Gratitude

Ti sono molto grato ...	I am very grateful to you ...
Le sono molto grato... [formal]	I am very grateful to you ...
Sei stato molto gentile...	You've been very kind...
E stato molto gentile... [formal]	It was very kind of you...
La ringrazio! [formal]	Thank you!
Grazie di tutto!	Thanks for everything!

13.14 Apologizing

Scusa!	Sorry!
Scusi! [formal]	Sorry!
Scusami (tanto)!	I am so sorry!
Mi scuso per ...	I apologize for ...
Mi dispiace!	I am sorry!

13.15 Expressing Indifference

Non mi interessa!	I don't care!
Per me è lo stesso.	It's all the same to me.
Fai come vuoi!	Do as you like!

Continued

13.16 Suggesting A Course Of Action (Including The Speaker)

Andiamo ...?	Shall we go ...?
Potremmo ...	We could ...
Vieni con noi ...?	Will you come with us ...?
Ti andrebbe di ...?	Would you like to ...?
Le andrebbe di ... ? [formal]	Would you like to ...?

13.17 Requesting Others To Do Something

Potresti ...?	Could you ...?
Potrebbe ...? [formal]	Could you ...?
Ti spiacerebbe ...?	Would you mind...?
Le spiacerebbe ...? [formal]	Would you mind ...?
Le sarei molto grato se potesse ...	I would be very grateful if you could ...

13.18 Asking For Advice

Che ne pensi ...?	What do you think of ...?
Hai qualche idea?	Any ideas?
Che cosa faresti (al mio posto)?	What would you do (in my situation?)
Che cosa mi consigli?	What do you suggest?
Che cosa mi consiglia? [formal]	What would you suggest?

13.19 Advising Others (Not) To Do Something

Secondo me, dovresti ...	In my opinion, you should...
Ti consiglio ...	I suggest that you ...
Le consiglio ... [formal]	I suggest that you ...
(Non) dovresti ...	You should ... (You should not)...
Faresti meglio a ...	You'd better ...
Perché non ...?	Why not ...?

13.20 Giving And Seeking Permission To Do Something

Puoi ...	You can ...
Certamente!	Certainly!
Naturalmente!	Of course!
Posso ...?	May I ...?
Potrei ...?	Could I ...?
Ti dispiace se ...?	Do you mind if ...?
Le dispiace se ... ? [formal]	Do you mind if ...?

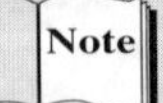

For a more detailed description of communicative functions and application in the appropriate context, see **Pronti .... Via! The Italian Handbook.**

14. "False Friends"

English/Italian "false friends" are words that are apparently similar but actually have different meanings.

e.g. LIBRERIA = bookshop; bookcase LIBRARY = biblioteca

Here follows a list of some common "false friends". If you learn them, you will be able to avoid some of the biggest pitfalls in oral and, more particularly, reading comprehension.

ITALIAN	ENGLISH
ARGOMENTO = subject, topic, point	ARGUMENT = discussione, controversia
ASSUMERE = to take on, to engage	TO ASSUME = supporre, assumere
ATTUALMENTE = at present, at the moment	ACTUALLY = realmente, effettivamente, in effetti, ...
CANTINA = cellar	CANTEEN = mensa, portaposate
COLLEGIO = boarding school	COLLEGE = 'college', università, politecnico, ...
COMPLESSIONE = constitution	COMPLEXION = carnagione, aspetto
CONFETTI = sugar-coated almonds	CONFETTI = coriandoli
CONFIDENZA = familiarity, intimacy	CONFIDENCE = fiducia, sicurezza (di sé), confidenza
CONVENIENTE = suitable, cheap, advantageous	CONVENIENT = comodo
EDUCAZIONE = (good) manners, upbringing	EDUCATION = istruzione, educazione
EVENTUALMENTE = perhaps, if necessary	EVENTUALLY = alla fine, in conclusione, finalmente
FACILITÀ = ease, facility	FACILITIES = attrezzature
FATTORIA = farm	FACTORY = fabbrica
MAGAZZINO = warehouse, department store	MAGAZINE = rivista, periodico
MORBIDO = soft; delicate	MORBID = morboso
PARENTE = relative	PARENT = genitore
PAVIMENTO = floor	PAVEMENT = marciapiede
PETROLIO = petroleum, crude oil	PETROL = benzina
POSSIBILMENTE = if possible	POSSIBLY = può darsi, forse, ...
REGISTRAZIONE = recording	REGISTRATION = iscrizione
RUMORE = noise	RUMOUR = voce, diceria
SENSIBILE = sensitive	SENSIBLE = sensato, ragionevole
SOPPORTARE = to stand, to bear	TO SUPPORT = mantenere, sostenere, tifare.

15. VOCABULARY

(R) = Receptive: is used to indicate words which only need to be understood for reading and listening rather than for active use in conversation. Basic level words followed by (R) should however be used actively at the higher level.

Higher level Italian words appear in bold.

*In general nouns ending in -**o** are masculine, those ending in -**a** are feminine. Irregular nouns are indicated by (m) when masculine, (f) when feminine. Singular nouns ending in -**e** can be masculine or feminine and are indicated accordingly by (m) or (f). Other abbreviations used are (pl.) for plural and (sing.) for singular.*

VOCABULARY LISTS BY TOPIC

PERSONAL IDENTIFICATION

Name

chi?	*who?*
chiamarsi	*to be called*
cognome (m)	*surname (R)*
compilare	*to fill in*
essere	*to be*
firma	*signature (R)*
firmare	*to sign (R)*
identità	*identity*
in stampatello	*in block letters (R)*
modulo	*form (R)*
nome (m)	*name*
riempire	*to fill in*
ripetere	*to repeat*
scrivere	*to write*
signora	*Mrs., Madam*
signore (m)	*Mr., Sir*
signorina	*Miss, Madam*

Home Address

abitare	*to live, to dwell*
appartamento	*flat*
ascensore (m)	*lift*
casa	*home, house*
codice postale (m)	*post code (R)*
corso	*main street*
destra	*right*
indirizzo	*address*
numero	*number*
paese (m)	*country, village*
palazzo	*building, mansion, block of flats*
piano	*floor, storey (R)*
piazza	*square*
primo	*first*
provincia	*province (R)*
regione (f)	*region*
sinistra	*left*
via	*road, street*
viale (m)	*avenue*

Telephone

dare	*to give*
fare il numero	*to dial*
gettone (m)	*token*
inserire	*to insert*
mettere	*to put*
numero	*number*
prefisso	*area code (telephone) (R)*
telefonare	*to telephone*

Age and Birthday

anni	*years*
anziano	*old, elderly*
avere	*to have*
compleanno	*birthday*
data di nascita	*date of birth (R)*
essere nato	*to have been born*
età	*age*
gennaio, ecc.	*January , etc.*
già	*already*
giovane	*young*
lunedì, ecc.	*Monday, etc*
luogo di nascita	*place of birth (R)*
maggiore	*older, elder (R)*
mese (m)	*month*
minore	*younger (R)*
quanti	*how many*
undicenne, ecc ...	*eleven year old, etc ...*
vecchio	*old*

Vocabulary

Nationality and country of residence

America	*America*
americano	*American*
Australia	*Australia*
australiano	*Australian*
bandiera	*flag*
belga	*Belgian*
Belgio	*Belgium*
britannico	*British*
carta di identità	*identity card*
danese	*Danish*
Danimarca	*Denmark*
dove?	*where?*
Europa	*Europe*
europeo	*European*
francese	*French*
Francia	*France*
Galles	*Wales*
gallese	*Welsh*
Germania	*Germany*
Gran Bretagna	*Great Britain*
Grecia	*Greece*
greco	*Greek*
Irlanda	*Ireland*
irlandese	*Irish*
Italia	*Italy*
Italiani	*the Italians*
italiano	*Italian*
lussemburghese	*Luxemburger*
Lussemburgo	*Luxemburg*
nato	*born*
nazione (f)	*nation*
Olanda	*Holland*
olandese	*Dutch*
passaporto	*passport*
Portogallo	*Portugal*
portoghese	*Portuguese*
residenza	*residence (R)*
Russia	*Russia*
russo	*Russian*
Scozia	*Scotland*
scozzese	*Scottish*
Spagna	*Spain*
spagnolo	*Spanish*
straniero	*foreigner*
tedesco	*German*

Occupations

assistente di volo (m/f)	*steward, stewardess*
autista (m/f)	*driver*
avvocato	*lawyer*
bene	*well*
cameriere (m)	*waiter*
casalinga	*housewife*
commerciante (m/f)	*trader*
commercio	*trade*
commesso	*shop-assistant*
dentista (m/f)	*dentist*
direttore (m)	*manager*
disoccupato	*unemployed*
ditta	*firm, company*
diventare	*to become*
dottore (m)	*doctor*
essere	*to be*
fabbrica	*factory (R)*
farmacista (m/f)	*chemist, pharmacist*
fattoria	*farm (R)*
guadagnare	*to earn*
impiegato	*employee*
infermiere (m)	*male nurse*
infermiera	*nurse*
insegnante (m/f)	*teacher*
interessante	*interesting*
lavorare	*to work*
lavoro	*job, work*
macellaio	*butcher*
maestro	*teacher (primary)*
magazzino	*store, warehouse*
male	*badly*
meccanico	*mechanic*
medico	*doctor*
negozio	*shop*
operaio	*workman*
padrone (m)	*owner*
paga	*pay, salary*
parrucchiere (m)	*hairdresser*
pizzeria	*'pizzeria'*
poliziotto	*policeman*
posizione (f)	*position*
professione (f)	*occupation, profession*
professore (m)	*teacher, professor*
proprietario	*owner*
salario	*wage*

Vocabulary

segretario	*secretary*
stipendio	*salary*
studente (m)	*student*
tassista (m/f)	*taxi-driver*
trovare un impiego	*to find a job*
ufficio	*office*

Likes and Dislikes

amare	*to love, to like*
andare matto per	*to be crazy about (R)*
favorito	*favourite*
migliore	*better*
molto	*much, very*
noioso	*boring*
non posso vedere	*I cannot stand/bear (R)*
odiare	*to hate*
ottimo	*very good, excellent*
peggiore	*worse*
piacere	*to like*
poco	*a little*
preferire	*to prefer*
tanto	*a lot*
volere	*to want*

General descriptions

Sex

bambino	*child*
donna	*woman*
femmina	*female*
figlio	*son*
maschio	*male*
ragazza	*girl*
ragazzo	*boy*
signorina	*young lady*
uomo	*man*

Marital status

celibe (m)	*single (R)*
congratularsi con	*to congratulate*
coniugato	*married (R)*
divorziato	*divorced*
fidanzarsi	*to become engaged*
fidanzato	*fiancé*
marito	*husband*
moglie	*wife*
nubile (f)	*single (R)*
scapolo	*bachelor*
separato	*separated*
sposarsi	*to get married*
sposato	*married*
sposo	*bridegroom*
stato civile	*marital status (R)*
vedovo	*widower*

Physical Appearance

a mio parere	*in my opinion*
alto	*tall*
anziano	*old, elderly*
azzurro	*light blue, azure (R)*
baffi (m, pl.)	*moustache (R)*
barba	*beard*
basso	*short*
bellezza	*beauty*
bello	*beautiful, handsome*
ben vestito	*well dressed*
bianco	*white*
biondo	*fair, blonde*
bocca	*mouth*
brutto	*ugly*
capelli (m, pl.)	*hair*
carino	*pretty*
carnagione (f)	*complexion*
castano	*brown, hazel*
chiaro	*fair*
corto	*short*
denti	*teeth*
elegante	*elegant; smart*
giovane	*young*
grasso	*fat*
grazioso	*pretty*
grosso	*big*
lisci (capelli ...)	*straight hair (R)*
lungo	*long*
magro	*thin*
naso	*nose*
nero	*black, dark*
occhi	*eyes*
occhiali	*glasses, spectacles*
ondulato	*wavy (R)*
orecchino	*earring*
orecchio	*ear*

Vocabulary

ricci (capelli ...)	*curly hair (R)*
robusto	*robust, sturdy*
snello	*slim*
somiglianza	*likeness*
sorriso	*smile*
sportivo	*sporty, casual (wear) (R)*
statura media	*average height*
vecchio	*old*
verde	*green (R)*

Character and Disposition

abbastanza	*rather, enough, quite*
allegro	*cheerful, merry*
antipatico	*unpleasant, disagreeable*
beneducato	*well mannered*
bravo	*good, clever*
buffo	*funny*
calmo	*calm*
comprensivo	*understanding*
contento	*happy, pleased*
cortese	*polite*
divertente	*amusing*
felice	*happy*
geloso	*jealous*
gentile	*kind*
intelligente	*intelligent*
maleducato	*bad mannered*
meraviglioso	*wonderful*
molto	*much, very*
nervoso	*irritable, nervous*
noioso	*boring*
onesto	*honest*
orgoglioso	*proud*
pazzo	*crazy*
pigro	*lazy*
piuttosto	*rather*
serio	*serious*
severo	*severe, strict*
simpatico	*nice*
studioso	*studious*
stupido	*stupid*
superbo	*proud, haughty*
timido	*shy, timid*
triste	*sad*
vivace	*vivacious, lively*

FAMILY

Members

amico	*friend*
andare a trovare	*to go and see, to visit*
avere	*to have*
babbo	*dad*
baciare	*to kiss*
bacio	*kiss*
bambino	*child*
cognato	*brother-in-law*
conoscere	*to know*
cugino	*cousin*
famiglia	*family*
figlio	*son*
figlio unico	*only son*
fratello	*brother*
gemelli	*twins*
genitore (m)	*parent*
giovane	*young*
grande	*big, grown-up*
insieme	*together*
madre (f)	*mother*
maggiore	*older*
mamma	*mummy*
marito	*husband*
matrimonio	*marriage, wedding*
minore	*younger*
moglie (f)	*wife*
nipote (m/f)	*nephew, niece, grand-son, grand-daughter*
nonno	*grand-father*
nozze (f, pl.)	*wedding*
numeroso	*numerous; large*
padre (m)	*father*
papà	*daddy*
parente (m/f)	*relative*
piccolo	*small*
presentare	*to introduce*
quanti	*how many*
ragazzo	*boy, boy-friend*
ragazza	*girl, girl-friend*
rassomigliare a	*to look like*
sorella	*sister*
spesso	*often*
suocero	*father-in-law*
unire	*to unite*
zio	*uncle*

Family Pets

abbaiare	*to bark*
accarezzare	*to stroke*
affezionarsi	*to grow fond*
amare	*to love*
ammirare	*to admire*
animale (m)	*animal*
animali domestici	*pets*
avere paura di	*to be afraid of*
bello	*beautiful*
buono	*good*
canarino	*canary*
cane (m)	*dog*
cantare	*to sing*
cavallo	*horse*
criceto	*hamster (R)*
dare da mangiare	*to feed*
docile	*docile*
feroce	*ferocious, fierce*
gabbia	*cage*
gattino	*kitten*
gatto	*cat*
graffiare	*to scratch*
grande	*big*
grosso	*large*
miagolare	*to mew, to miaow (R)*
mordere	*to bite*
pesce (m)	*fish (R)*
piccolo	*small*
preferire	*to prefer*
tartaruga	*tortoise (R)*
temere	*to fear*
uccellino	*little bird*

HOUSE AND HOME

General

abitare	*to live*
affittare	*to let, to rent*
affitto	*rent*
aiuola	*flower-bed*
albero	*tree*
ammobiliato	*furnished (R)*
ampio	*large*
angolo	*corner (R)*
antico	*old, antique*
appartamento	*flat*
ascensore (m)	*lift*
balcone (m)	*balcony*
bello	*beautiful*
ben tenuto	*well kept*
bosco	*wood*
brutto	*ugly*
calmo	*calm, quiet*
caminetto	*fire-place*
campanello	*bell*
cancello	*gate (R)*
caratteristico	*distinctive*
carino	*pretty*
caro	*dear, expensive*
casa	*home, house*
comodità	*comfort*
comodo	*comfortable*
comprare	*to buy*
cortile (m)	*court-yard*
davanti a	*opposite, in front of*
decorare	*to decorate*
dietro	*behind*
difficile	*difficult*
edificio	*building*
entrare	*to enter*
entrata	*entrance*
erba	*grass (R)*
facile	*easy*
fiore (m)	*flower*
garage (m)	*garage*
giardino	*garden*
grande	*big*
in fondo a	*at the end of*
inquilino	*tenant*
isolato	*isolated, remote*

Vocabulary

legno	*wood (R)*
località	*area*
lontano da	*far from*
moderno	*modern*
muro	*wall*
nuovo	*new*
padrone di casa (m)	*landlord, owner*
pagare l'affitto	*to pay the rent*
palazzo	*building, mansion, block of flats*
perfetto	*perfect*
piacere	*to like*
piano	*floor, storey*
pitturare	*to paint*
plastica	*plastic*
portachiavi (m)	*key-ring*
posate (f, pl.)	*cutlery*
prato	*lawn*
proprio	*own*
pulito	*clean*
quartiere (m)	*quarter, neighbourhood*
quasi	*almost*
roba	*stuff, things*
rumore (m)	*noise*
rumoroso	*noisy*
solaio	*loft; attic*
sopra	*on, over, above*
sotto	*under*
spazioso	*spacious*
specchio	*mirror*
sporco	*dirty*
stanza	*room*
stretto	*narrow*
suonare	*ring*
tetto	*roof*
trascurato	*neglected (R)*
traslocare	*to move (house) (R)*
veramente	*really*
vestire	*to dress*
vestirsi	*to get dressed*
vicino a	*near*
villa	*villa, house*
vista	*view*

Accommodation and Services

accendere	*to switch on*
acqua	*water*
(al piano) di sopra	*upstairs (R)*
(al piano) di sotto	*downstairs (R)*
al piano superiore	*on the upper floor*
al pianterreno	*on the ground floor*
al primo piano	*on the first floor*
aprire	*to open*
automobile (f)	*car*
balcone (m)	*balcony*
bottone/pulsante (m)	*button*
caldo	*hot*
camera (da letto)	*bedroom*
cantina	*cellar*
chiudere	*to shut*
confortevole	*comfortable*
cucina	*kitchen*
dormire	*to sleep*
elettricità	*electricity*
elettrico	*electric*
entrata	*entrance*
fiammifero	*match*
finestra	*window*
fornello	*cooker*
freddo	*cold*
funzionare	*to work, to function*
gabinetto	*toilet*
garage (m)	*garage*
ingresso	*entrance, hallway*
lavandino	*wash basin, sink*
macchina	*car, machine*
non funziona	*out of order*
porta	*door*
premere	*to press (R)*
riscaldamento centrale	*central heating*
rubinetto	*tap*
sala da pranzo	*dining room*
salotto	*sitting-room, drawing room*
scale (f, pl.)	*stairs*
soggiorno	*living-room*
spegnere	*to switch off*
stanza	*room*
(stanza da) bagno	*bathroom*
studio	*study*
tinello	*(small) dining-room*

Furniture, household equipment and appliances

apparecchiare *to lay the table*
armadio *wardrobe*
arredare *to furnish*
asciugamano *hand towel*
aspirapolvere (m) *vacuum-cleaner*
bagno (vasca da ...) *bath*
bicchiere (m) *glass*
bottiglia *bottle*
caffettiera *coffee pot*
casseruola *saucepan*
cassetto *drawer*
coltello *knife*
congelatore (m) *freezer*
coperta *cover, blanket*
cosa *thing*
credenza *sideboard*
cucchiaino *teaspoon, coffee-spoon*
cucchiaio *spoon*
cucina *kitchen*
cuscino *cushion, pillow*
dentifricio *toothpaste*
disco *disc, record*
divano *settee*
doccia *shower*
elettricità *electricity*
elettrico *electric*
elettrodomestici *electric household appliances*
federa *pillow-case*
forchetta *fork*
forno *oven*
fotografia *photograph*
frigorifero *refrigerator*
giradischi (m) *record player*
lampada *lamp*
lampadina *light bulb*
lavastoviglie (f) *dish-washer*
lavatrice (f) *washing machine*
legno *wood*
lenzuolo *sheet*
letto *bed*
libreria *bookcase (R)*
lucidatrice (f) *floor-polisher*
mobile (m) *piece of furniture (R)*
orologio *clock*
padella *pan*
paio *pair*
parecchi *many, several*
pattumiera *dustbin*
pentola *pot; pan (R)*
pianoforte (m) *piano*
piattino *saucer*
piatto *plate, dish*
piumino *duvet*
poltrona *arm-chair*
portacenere (m) *ash-tray*
quadro *picture*
radio (f) *radio*
registratore (m) *tape-recorder*
rotto *broken*
sapone (m) *soap*
scaffale (m) *shelf (R)*
sedia *chair*
soprammobile (m) *ornament*
sparecchiare *to clear the table*
spazzolino da denti *toothbrush*
sveglia *alarm clock*
tappeto *carpet*
tazza *cup*
tazzina *coffee-cup*
tegame *saucepan (R)*
teiera *tea-pot*
televisione (f) *television*
tende *curtains (R)*
tovaglia *table cloth*
tovagliolo *napkin, serviette (R)*
video registratore *video recorder*

Hospitality

accomodarsi *to sit down*
altrettanto (a te) *the same to you*
andare a trovare *to pay a visit*
approfittare *to take advantage of*
arrivederci *goodbye*
augurare *to wish*
aver bisogno di *to need*
compleanno *birthday*
contento *happy*
dire *to tell, to say*
dovere *to have to*
entrare *to enter*
fare visita *to pay a visit*

Vocabulary

gentile	*kind*
giornata	*day*
grazie	*thanks*
lieto	*glad, pleased*
molto	*much, very*
ospitalità	*hospitality*
partire	*to leave*
passare	*to pass, to spend*
per favore/piacere	*please*
prego!	*don't mention it!, you are welcome!*
salutare	*to greet*
sedersi	*to sit*
si accomodi	*take a seat*
tanto	*much*
trascorrere	*to spend, to pass*
volere	*to want, to wish*

Life at Home and Daily Routine

abitudine (f)	*habit*
aiutare	*to help*
alzarsi	*to get up*
andare bene	*to go well*
ascoltare	*to listen to*
aver bisogno di	*to need*
badare al bambino	*to babysit*
cena	*supper, evening meal, dinner*
ciascuno	*every, each, everyone*
comprare	*to buy*
cucinare	*to cook*
cucire	*to sew*
di mattina	*in the morning*
di solito	*usually*
dormire	*to sleep*
faccende (f, pl.)	*housework*
fare colazione	*to have breakfast*
fare i compiti	*to do (one's) homework*
fare la spesa	*to do the shopping*
finalmente	*at last*
giocare	*to play*
lavarsi	*to wash (oneself)*
lavorare	*to work*
leggere	*to read*
libro	*book*
mangiare	*to eat*
mercato	*market*
merenda	*(afternoon) snack (R)*
mettere via	*to put away*
noia	*boredom*
ora	*hour, now*
passatempo	*pastime, hobby*
pettinarsi	*to comb one's hair*
pranzo	*lunch, main meal*
preparare da mangiare	*to prepare a meal*
pulire	*to clean*
spolverare	*to dust*
stirare	*to iron*
supermercato	*supermarket*
svegliarsi	*to wake up*
volentieri	*of course, with pleasure, willingly*

Spare time job and spending money

abbastanza	*enough*
avere	*to have*
bicicletta	*bicycle*
cominciare	*to begin*
dare	*to give*
desiderare	*to wish, to want, to like*
di buon' ora	*early*
fare	*to make, to do*
finire	*to finish*
giorno	*day*
guadagnare	*to earn*
impiegarsi	*to be employed, to get a job*
lavorare	*to work*
mancare	*to lack*
mattina	*morning*
mese (m)	*month*
pagare	*to pay*
permettersi	*to take the liberty*
pomeriggio	*afternoon*
quanto	*how much*
risparmiare	*to save*
sera	*evening*
settimana	*week*
soldi da spendere	*spending money*
soldi (m, pl.)	*money*
spendere	*to spend*
spiccioli (m, pl.)	*loose change*
sterlina	*pound (sterling)*
tardi	*late*
troppo	*too much*

GEOGRAPHICAL SURROUNDINGS AND WEATHER

Geographical Surroundings

Location

a	*at, to, in*
abitante (m)	*inhabitant*
abitare	*to live*
accanto a	*by, next to, beside*
all'aria aperta	*in the open air*
andare; (... a fare)	*to go; (to ... and do)*
andarsene	*to go away*
avviarsi	*to set off, to be about to*
avvicinarsi a	*to approach*
bordo	*edge*
c'è, ci sono	*there is, there are*
camminare	*to walk*
campagna (in ...)	*country (in the ...)*
capitale (f)	*capital*
centro	*centre*
chilometro	*kilometre*
cielo	*sky*
cima; (in ... a)	*peak; (on the top of)*
circa	*about*
città (in ...)	*city, town (in the ...)*
da	*from, to, by*
davanti a	*in front of; opposite*
destra (a ...)	*right (on the ...)*
di	*of*
dietro (a)	*behind*
dintorni	*surroundings*
dirigersi	*to make for*
distante da	*far from*
distanza	*distance*
distare	*to be, (... a long way from)*
dove, dov'è	*where, where is*
dovunque	*everywhere*
entro	*within, into*
esistere	*to exist, to be*
est (m)	*east*
fare	*to do, to make*
fino a	*as far as*
fondo (in ... a)	*at the end of*
fronte (di ... a)	*in front of*
fuori (di ...)	*outside*
già	*already*
girare	*to go around, to turn*
giro	*tour*
gita	*excursion, trip*
giù	*down*
in	*in, to, at, by*
intorno a	*around*
laggiù	*down there*
lassù	*up there*
là, lì	*there*
località	*locality, place*
lontananza	*distance*
lontano da	*far from*
luogo	*place*
mare; (al ...)	*sea; (at the seaside)*
mezzo (in ... a)	*middle (in the ... of)*
mezzogiorno	*midday*
miglio; (miglia)	*mile; (miles)*
mille	*thousand*
mondo	*world*
montagna (in ...)	*mountain (in the ...s)*
nord (m)	*north*
ovest (m)	*west*
parte; (da questa ...; da nessuna ...)	*side (on this side; nowhere)*
passato	*past*
passeggiare	*to stroll, to walk*
passeggiata	*stroll, walk*
periferia (in ...)	*suburb (in the ...)*
posto	*place*
prendere	*to take*
quaggiù	*down here*
quanto (... ci vuole?)	*how long (... does it take?)*
quanto	*how much*
quassù	*up here*
qui, qua	*here*
regione (f)	*region*
risalire	*to go up again*
ritornare	*to return*
salire	*to go up*
salita	*climb*
scendere	*to descend, to go down*
sinistra (a...)	*left (on the ...)*
sito	*place; situated*
situato	*situated*
situazione (f)	*situation*
sopra	*over, above, on*
sotto	*under, beneath, below*
sperduto	*out of the way (R)*

Vocabulary

su	*on; over; above*
sud (m)	*south*
terra	*earth, ground, land*
tornare	*to return*
tra/fra	*among; between*
trovarsi	*to find oneself*
vedere	*to see*
venire	*to come*
verso	*towards*
vicino a	*near, next to*
visitare	*to visit*
vista	*view*
vivere	*to live*

Amenities/features of interest

abbastanza	*rather; enough; quite*
aeroporto	*airport*
albergo	*hotel*
albero	*tree*
alto	*high*
altro	*other*
animale (m)	*animal*
annoiarsi	*to be bored*
antico	*ancient*
appena	*just, hardly*
architettura	*architecture*
abbazia	*abbey*
banca	*bank*
basso	*low*
bello	*beautiful*
bene	*well*
bosco	*wood*
brutto	*ugly*
buono	*good*
calmo	*calm*
campeggio	*camping site*
campo	*field, camp*
canale (m)	*canal*
carta geografica	*map*
casa colonica	*farmhouse*
castello	*castle*
cattedrale (f)	*cathedral*
chiasso	*noise (R)*
chiesa	*church*
chiuso	*closed*
cinema (m)	*cinema*
circostante	*surrounding*
colle (m)	*hill, pass*
collina	*hill*
collinoso	*hilly (R)*
coltivare	*to cultivate*
commerciale	*commercial, trade*
concerto	*concert*
conoscere	*to know*
così	*thus*
costa	*coast, shore*
costruito	*built*
credere	*to believe*
discoteca	*discotheque*
divertimento	*amusement*
divertirsi	*to amuse oneself*
dovere	*to have to*
duomo	*cathedral*
edificio	*building*
epoca	*age, epoch*
erba	*grass*
fabbrica	*factory*
fattoria	*farm*
fiore (m)	*flower*
fiume (m)	*river*
fontana	*fountain*
foresta	*forest*
fragore (m)	*noise*
fragoroso	*noisy (R)*
fresco	*fresh*
giardino	*garden*
goder(si)	*to enjoy (oneself)*
grande	*big, large*
grazie a	*thanks to*
importante	*important*
incantevole	*enchanting, delightful*
indicare	*to point out, to show*
industria	*industry*
industriale	*industrial*
insetto	*insect*
interamente	*entirely*
interessante	*interesting*
isola	*island*
lago	*lake*
largo	*wide, large*
lato	*side*
lungo	*long*
lupo	*wolf*
ma	*but*
malgrado	*in spite of*
medievale	*medieval*
meglio	*better, best*

meno — *less*
migliaia — *thousands*
migliore — *better, best*
moderno — *modern*
molto — *much, very much*
monotono — *monotonous, dull*
monte (m) — *mountain*
monumento — *monument*
municipale — *municipal, local government*
municipio — *town-hall*
museo — *museum*
negozio — *shop*
nessuno — *no-one*
niente — *nothing*
noioso — *boring*
nuovo — *new*
ogni — *every*
opera — *opera*
orto — *vegetable garden*
ospedale (m) — *hospital*
osservare — *to observe, to watch*
paesaggio — *landscape, scenery*
palazzo — *building, block of flats; palace*
panorama (m) — *view, panorama*
parco — *park*
parecchio — *quite a lot of*
parere — *to seem*
pendio — *slope*
però — *however*
pesca — *fishing*
pesce (m) — *fish*
piacere — *to like*
(mi piace, mi piacciono) *(I like it, I like them)*
piacevole — *pleasant*
pianta — *plant*
picco — *peak*
piccolo — *small*
pietra — *stone*
piscina — *swimming pool*
pittoresco — *picturesque*
più — *more*
poco, (pochi) — *little, (few)*
podere (m) — *farm*
ponte (m) — *bridge*
porto — *port*
prato — *meadow, lawn*
presso — *close to, near (R)*
profondo — *deep*
proprio — *just*
pubblico — *public*
pulito — *clean*
qualche — *some, a few*
quale — *what, which*
quartiere (m) — *district*
quasi — *almost*
raro — *unusual, uncommon*
ripido — *steep*
riva — *shore*
riviera — *coast, 'riviera'*
roccia — *rock*
roccioso — *rocky (R)*
rumore (m) — *noise*
rumoroso — *noisy*
rurale — *rural*
sapere — *to know*
sasso — *stone*
scampagnata — *trip to the country*
scuola — *school*
secolo — *century*
sembrare — *to seem, to look like*
sereno — *clear, fine*
settentrionale — *northern*
siepe (f) — *hedge*
sommità — *top*
spettacolo — *show, sight*
spiaggia — *beach*
sporco — *dirty*
sport (m) — *sport*
sportivo — *sporting*
stadio — *stadium*
stazione (f) — *station*
stesso — *same*
stile (m) — *style*
storico — *historic*
strada — *street, road*
stretto — *narrow*
stupendo — *stupendous, marvellous*
suono — *sound*
tanto — *so much, a lot of*
teatro — *theatre*
terreno — *ground, soil*
tranquillo — *quiet, calm*
tuttavia — *nevertheless, yet*
tutto — *all, everything*
uccello — *bird*

Vocabulary

valle (f) *valley*
vecchio *old*
veduta/vista *view, sight*
viale (m) *avenue*
villaggio *village*

Weather

afoso *sultry*
alba *dawn*
anno *year*
asciutto *dry (R)*
atmosfera *atmosphere*
autunno *autumn*
aver caldo/freddo ecc. *to be hot, cold etc.*
bagnato; (... fradicio) *wet; (soaked) (R)*
bianco *white*
bollettino; (... meteorologico) *bulletin; (weather forecast)*
brezza *breeze*
buio *dark*
cadere *to fall*
caldo *hot*
cambiamento *change*
cambiare *to change*
caso *chance, case*
catinelle (piove a ...) *it rains cats and dogs (R)*
che tempo fa? *what's the weather like?*
chiaro *clear*
cielo *sky*
clima (m) *climate*
cominciare; (... a fare) *to begin; (... to)*
coperto *cloudy, overcast*
correre *to run*
domani *tomorrow*
dopodomani *the day after tomorrow*
estate (f) *summer*
far bel tempo/bello *to be good weather/fine*
brutto tempo *to be bad weather*
caldo *to be hot*
freddo *to be cold*
fresco *cool*
fresco *fresh*
fulmine (m) *lightning*
fuori *outside*
gelare *to freeze*
generale (in ...) *in general*
generalmente *generally*
ghiaccio *ice*
giorno/giornata *day*
gradi (centigradi) *degrees (centigrade)*
grandine (f) *hail*
ieri *yesterday*
impermeabile (m) *raincoat*
indossare *to put on*
inverno *winter*
l'altro ieri *the day before yesterday*
lampeggiare *to lighten (R)*
lampo *flash of lightning*
limpido *clear, limpid (R)*
luce (f) *light*
luna *moon*
magnifico *magnificent, splendid*
mattina/mattinata *morning*
mese (m) *month*
metter(si) *to change*
miglioramento *improvement*
migliorare *to improve*
mite *mild (R)*
nebbia *fog*
nero *black*
neve (f) *snow*
nevicare *to snow*
nevoso *snowy (R)*
notte (f) *night*
nuvola *cloud*
occhiali, (... da sole) *spectacles, (sun-glasses)*
oggi *today*
ogni *every*
ombra *shadow, shade*
passato *past*
peggiorare *to deteriorate*
pioggia *rain*
piovere *to rain*
piovigginare *to drizzle (R)*
piovoso *rainy (R)*
poco (fra ...) *in a short while*
pomeriggio *afternoon*
precipitazione (f) *precipitation (R)*
presto *soon*
prevedere *to forecast*
previsioni del tempo *weather forecast*
previsioni meteorologiche *weather forecast*

primavera *spring*
prossimo *next*
quindicina; (... di giorni) *about fifteen; (a fortnight)*
rado (di ...) *seldom*
raramente *rarely*
ripararsi *to shelter*
riparo *shelter*
rovescio *downpour*
scintillare *to sparkle*
scivolare *to slip*
scorso *last, past*
scroscio *downpour*
scuro *dark*
sdraiarsi *to lie down*
secco *dry*
sedia a sdraio *deck-chair*
segnare *to indicate*
sempre *always*
senza *without*
sera/serata *evening*
sereno *clear, cloudless*
settimana *week*
sole (m) *sun*
soleggiato *sunny*
solito; (di ...) *usual; (usually)*
splendido *splendid*
stagione (f) *season*
stella *star*
stufo *fed up*
sudare *to sweat*
sudore (m) *sweat*
tempaccio *nasty weather (R)*
temperatura *temperature*
tempesta *storm*
tempestoso *stormy*
tempo *time, weather*
temporale (m) *thunder storm*
termometro *thermometer*
tirare *to blow*
tramonto *sunset*
troppo *too much*
tuonare *to thunder*
umidità *dampness; humidity*
umido *damp*
variabile *variable*
variazione *variation*
vento *wind*
visibilità *visibility*
zero; (sopra/sotto...) *zero; (above/below...)*

TRAVEL AND TRANSPORT

General

affrettarsi *to hurry*
andare *to go*
a piedi *on foot*
arrivare *to arrive*
autobus (m) *bus*
automobile (f) *car*
autostop; (fare l'...) *hitch-hiking; (to hitch-hike)*
bicicletta *bicycle*
casa *house*
comodo *comfortable*
di buon' ora *early*
diretto *direct*
entrare *to enter*
fretta (aver ...) *hurry (to be in a ...)*
lavoro *work*
macchina *machine, car*
metropolitana *underground railway*
mezzo *means*
momento *moment*
moneta *coin*
motoscafo *motor boat*
officina *workshop*
partire *to leave*
pratico *practical*
preferire *to prefer*
presto *soon*
rapidamente *rapidly; quickly*
restare *to stay*
rimanere *to stay*
ritardo; (in ...) *delay; (late)*
ritornare *to return*
salire *to get on, to go up*
scendere *to get off, to go down*
scuola *school*
sempre *always*
solito; (di ...) *usual; (usually)*
spesso *often*
spiccioli (m, pl.) *loose change*
stesso *same*

Vocabulary

tardi *late*
tornare *to return*
trasporto *transport*
ufficio *office*
uscire *to go out*
viaggiare *to travel*
viaggio *journey*

Finding the way

accanto a *next to, near*
aiutare *to help*
allora *then*
altrove *elsewhere*
angolo; (... della strada) *corner; street corner*
appena *hardly, as soon as*
attraversare *to cross,*
avanti *in front of, ahead*
breve *brief, short*
c'è, ci sono *there is, there are*
caffè (m) *cafè*
camminare *to walk*
capire *to understand*
castello *castle*
centro *centre*
chiesa *church*
chilometro *kilometre*
città *city, town*
come *how*
commissariato *police station*
comunque *anyhow, however (R)*
continuare *to continue*
corso *avenue, main street*
davanti a *in front of, opposite*
dentro *inside*
destinazione (f) *destination*
destra; (a ...) *right; (on the ...)*
dietro (... a) *behind*
direzione (f) *direction*
diritto *straight*
discoteca *discotheque*
distanza *distance*
domandare *to ask*
dopo *after*
dove, dov'è? *where, where is?*
edificio *building*
ente per il turismo (m) *tourist board*
entrata *entry, entrance; admission*
entro *within*
essere *to be*
est (m) *east*
fermata (di autobus) *bus stop*
fine (f) *end*
fino a *as far as*
fondo (in ... a) *at the bottom of, at the end of*
fronte (di ... a) *in front of*
garage (m) *garage*
grazie! *thank you!*
incontrare *to meet*
incontro; (andare ... a) *meeting; (to meet)*
incrocio *crossing, crossroads*
informare *to inform*
informazione (f) *information*
ingresso *entrance*
laggiù *down there*
lato *side*
là *there*
lontano (da) *far from*
lungo *long, along*
marciapiede (m) *pavement*
mercato *market*
municipio *town hall*
museo *museum*
nessuno *no-one*
niente; (di ...!) *nothing; (don't mention it!)*
nord (m) *north*
ostello della gioventù *youth hostel*
ovest (m) *west*
parti; (da queste ...) *parts; (around here)*
passante (m/f) *passer-by*
passare *to pass*
passeggiare *to stroll, to walk*
passi (a due ... da qui) *a stone's throw from here*
pedone (m) *pedestrian*
perdersi *to get lost*
pianta; (... della città) *map; (... of the town)*
piazza *square*
piedi (a ...) *on foot*
piscina *swimming pool*
poi *then*
posto *place*

potere *to be able*
prego! *don't mention it!*
prendere *to take*
primo, secondo, ecc. *first, second, etc.*
proprio *just*
qualche *some, a few*
quale *which*
questura *police headquarters*
qui *here*
ringraziare *to thank*
ripetere *to repeat*
ristorante (m) *restaurant*
salire *to get on, to go up*
scendere *to get off, to go down*
scusi! *excuse me!*
segnale (m) *signal, sign*
seguire *to follow*
semaforo *traffic lights*
senso, (a ... unico) *direction, (one-way)*
servizio *service*
sindaco *mayor*
sinistra; (a ...) *left; (on the...)*
stadio *stadium*
stazione (f) *station*
strada *road, street*
subito *at once*
sud (m) *south*
trattoria *'trattoria', (small) restaurant*
trovarsi *to be, to be situated*
tutto *all*
ufficio postale *post office*
uscita *exit*
via *road, street*
vicino a *near, close to, by*
vietato *prohibited*
volere; (quanto ci vuole per ...?) *to take; (how long does it take to ...?)*

Public Transport

aperto *open*
arrivo; (in ...) *arrival; (arriving)*
aspettare *to wait*
assicurare *to assure, to ensure*
bagaglio *luggage*
banchina *quay*
bar (m) *bar*
biglietteria *ticket office*
biglietto (... semplice) *ticket (single ...)*
biglietto di andata e ritorno *return ticket*
binario *platform*
bisognare *to need*
cambiare *to change*
camion (m) *lorry*
capolinea (m) *terminus*
caro *expensive*
classe (f) *class*
coda/fila; (fare la ...) *queue; (to queue up)*
coincidenza *connection*
comprare *to buy*
conducente (m/f) *driver*
controllore (m) *inspector (R)*
corriera *coach*
costare *to cost*
cuccetta *couchette*
depositare *to deposit*
deposito; (... bagagli) *deposit; (left luggage office)*
diretto a ... *going to ... (R)*
domandare *to ask*
facchino *porter*
facoltativo *optional*
fare *to make, to do*
fermarsi *to stop*
fermata *stop*
ferrovia *railway*
filobus (m) *trolley bus*
finestrino *window*
fumare *to smoke*
fumatori, (non ...) *smoker, (non-smoker)*
gabinetto *toilet*
gente (f, sing.) *people*
in anticipo *early*
in piedi *standing*
in ritardo *late*
lento *slow*
libero *free*
linea *line*
locomotiva *locomotive*
mancia *tip*
mezzanotte (f) *midnight*
mezzogiorno *midday*
nave (f) *ship*
numero *number*

Vocabulary

obbligatorio *obligatory*
occupato *engaged, occupied*
oggetti smarriti *lost property*
ora *time, hour*
orario *timetable*
pagare *to pay*
partenza; (in ...) *departure; (leaving)*
partire *to leave*
passeggero *passenger*
perdere *to lose, to miss*
pericolo *danger*
pericoloso *dangerous*
periferia *suburb*
pianta *map*
portabagagli *porter (R)*
portare *to carry*
portiera *door*
posto *place*
prendere *to take*
prenotare *to book*
prenotazione (f) *reservation*
prezzo *price*
primo *first*
prossimo *next*
proveniente da ... *coming from ... (R)*
pullman (m) *coach*
quale *which*
quanto *how much*
quarto *quarter*
rapido *'special express train'*
raramente *rarely*
ridotto *reduced*
rischio *risk*
riservare *to reserve*
ritardare *to delay*
sacco *bag*
sala d'aspetto *waiting room*
salire *to get on*
scendere *to get off*
scompartimento *compartment*
sedersi *to sit down*
seduto *seated*
sobborghi *suburbs*
soppresso *cancelled (R)*
sporgersi *to lean out*
sportello *door*
stare *to stay*
stazione (f) *station*
supplemento *supplement*
tassì *taxi*
tram (m) *tram*
treno, (... locale, diretto, espresso) *train, (slow, fast, express ...)*
turista (m/f) *tourist*
ufficio informazioni *information office*
ultimo *last*
vagone letto (m) *sleeping car, sleeper*
valigia *suitcase*
vettura *coach, carriage*
viaggiatore (m) *traveller*
vicino *near*
vietato *prohibited*

Travel by Air/Sea

(niente da ...) *(nothing to ...)*
aereo; (... a reazione) *aeroplane; (jet)*
aliscafo *hydrofoil*
aprire *to open*
assistente di volo (m/f) *steward, stewardess*
atterrare *to land (R)*
battello *boat*
carta d'imbarco *boarding pass (R)*
chiedere *to ask*
chiudere *to close*
cintura di sicurezza *safety belt (R)*
controllo *check*
crociera *cruise*
decollare *to take off (R)*
dichiarare (qualche cosa da ...) *declare (something to...)*
dogana *customs*
doganiere, guardia di finanzia *customs officer*
frontiera *frontier*
'hostess' *air hostess*
hovercraft (m) *hovercraft (R)*
imbarcare *to embark, board (R)*
nave (f) *ship*
passaporto *passport*
passare *to pass*
pilota *pilot*
porto *port, harbour*
sbarcare *to disembark (R)*
traghetto (nave ...) *ferry (boat)*

transatlantico *(transatlantic) liner*
traversata *crossing (R)*
uscita *exit, gate (R)*
volare *to fly*
volo charter *charter flight (R)*
volo di linea *scheduled flight (R)*
volo *flight*

Private Transport

agente di polizia *policeman*
allacciare *to fasten*
andare *to go*
aria *air*
arrestare *to stop*
assicurazione *insurance*
autista (m/f) *driver*
autostrada *motorway*
batteria *battery*
benzina *petrol*
bicicletta *bicycle*
cambio *change gear*
camion (m) *lorry*
candela *spark plug (R)*
carta (... automobilistica) *map (road ...)*
carta verde *green card (R)*
cartello, (... indicatore) *sign, (direction sign)*
casco *helmet (R)*
casello (di autostrada) *tollgate (R)*
cintura di sicurezza *seat belt*
circolazione vietata *no through road (R)*
codice della strada (m) *highway code*
cofano *bonnet*
controllare *to control, to check*
copertone (m) *tyre*
curva; (... a sinistra) *bend; (left turn)*
dare la precedenza *to give way*
diritto *right; straight on*
disco orario *parking disc (R)*
distributore (di benzina) (m) *petrol pump*
diversione/deviazione (f) *diversion*
documenti *documents (vehicle ...)*
dovere *duty*
fare *to make, to do*
filare *to go*
forare *to have a puncture (R)*
foratura *puncture (R)*
frenare *to brake*
freno *brake*
frizione *clutch*
furgone (m) *van (R)*
gomma *tyre,*
gonfiare *to inflate (R)*
gratuito, (ingresso ...) *free, (admission ...)*
guasto *breakdown, failure*
guidare *to drive*
incidente (m) *accident*
incrocio *crossroads*
ingorgo *(traffic) jam (R)*
lavaggio *washing; car wash*
lavori in corso *work in progress*
libretto (di circolazione) *log book (R)*
limite di velocità (m) *speed limit*
litro *litre*
macchina *car*
marca *make*
moto (cicletta) (f) *motorcycle*
motore (m) *engine*
multa *fine*
nafta *diesel (R)*
noleggiare *to hire*
nolo (prendere a ...) *hire (to ...)*
numero *number*
olio *oil*
ore di punta *rush hours (R)*
panne (in ...) *breakdown (R)*
parcheggiare *to park*
parchimetro *parking meter (R)*
patente (f) *driving licence*
pedaggio *toll*
pezzi di ricambio *spare parts*
pieno; (fare il ...) *full; (to fill it up)*
pneumatico *tyre*
Polizia Urbana *'City Police' (R)*
poliziotto *policeman*
pompa (di benzina) *petrol pump*
posteggio *parking space*
pressione (f) *pressure*
rallentare *to slow down*
riparare *to mend*
ruota *wheel*
scontro *bump, collision*
semaforo *traffic lights*
senso (a ... unico) *one way*
senza piombo (benzina) *unleaded (petrol) (R)*

Vocabulary

sorpassare	*to overtake*
sosta	*parking*
statale (strada ...)	*main road*
super (benzina)	*super, premium fuel*
targa	*number plate*
traffico	*traffic*
veloce	*fast*
velocità	*speed*
verificare	*to check*
vespa	*'vespa', motor scooter*
vigile (urbano) (m)	*'traffic policeman'*
volante (m)	*steering wheel*
vuoto	*empty*

Abbreviations

A Autostrada *Motorway*
A.C.I. Automobile Club d'Italia *Italian Automobile Club*
A.R. Andata e Ritorno (biglietto di...) *Return ticket*
A.Z. Alitalia *Italian Airline*
D Diretto *'Fast Train'*
F.S. Ferrovie dello Stato *State Railways*
FF.SS. Ferrovie dello Stato *State Railways*
MM Metropolitana Milanese *Milan Underground*
SP Strada Provinciale *Provincial Road*
SS Strada Statale *Main Road*

CC Carabinieri *'Police Force' (Carabinieri)*
POLFER Polizia Ferroviaria *Railway police*
POLSTRADA Polizia Stradale *Traffic/ highway police*
P.S. Pubblica Sicurezza *State Police*
VV.UU Vigili Urbani *'Traffic Police'*

Italian Number Plates: Letters used to indicate provinces

AG	Agrigento	**AL**	Alessandria
AN	Ancona	**AO**	Aosta
AP	Ascoli Piceno	**AQ**	Aquila
AR	Arezzo	**AT**	Asti
AV	Avellino	**BA**	Bari
BG	Bergamo	**BL**	Belluno
BN	Benevento	**BO**	Bologna
BR	Brindisi	**BS**	Brescia
BZ	Bolzano	**CA**	Cagliari
CB	Campobasso	**CE**	Caserta
CH	Chieti	**CL**	Caltanissetta
CN	Cuneo	**CO**	Como
CR	Cremona	**CS**	Cosenza
CT	Catania	**CZ**	Catanzaro
EN	Enna	**FE**	Ferrara
FG	Foggia	**FI**	Firenze
FO	Forlì	**FR**	Frosinone
GE	Genova	**GO**	Gorizia
GR	Grosseto	**IM**	Imperia
IS	Isernia	**LE**	Lecce
LI	Livorno	**LT**	Latina
LU	Lucca	**MC**	Macerata
ME	Messina	**MI**	Milano
MN	Mantova	**MO**	Modena
MS	Massa Carrara	**MT**	Matera
NA	Napoli	**NO**	Novara
NU	Nuoro	**OR**	Oristano
PA	Palermo	**PC**	Piacenza
PD	Padova	**PE**	Pescara
PG	Perugia	**PI**	Pisa
PN	Pordenone	**PR**	Parma
PS	Pesaro	**PT**	Pistoia
PV	Pavia	**PZ**	Potenza
RA	Ravenna	**RC**	Reggio Calabria
RE	Reggio Emilia	**RG**	Ragusa
RI	Rieti	**RO**	Rovigo
SA	Salerno	**SI**	Siena
SO	Sondrio	**SP**	La Spezia
SR	Siracusa	**SS**	Sassari
SV	Savona	**TA**	Taranto
TE	Teramo	**TN**	Trento
TO	Torino	**TP**	Trapani
TR	Terni	**TS**	Trieste
TV	Treviso	**UD**	Udine
VA	Varese	**VC**	Vercelli
VE	Venezia	**VI**	Vicenza
VR	Verona	**VT**	Viterbo
ROMA	Roma		

*****

A.M. Aeronautica Militare *Air Force*
E.I. Esercito Italiano *Italian Army*
M.M. Marina Militare *Navy*
R.S.M. Repubblica di San Marino *Republic of San Marino*

S.C.V. Stato Città del Vaticano *Vatican City*
V.F. Vigili del Fuoco *Fire Brigade*

HOLIDAYS

General

abbronzarsi *to get a tan*
abbronzato *sun-tanned*
affittare *to rent, to hire*
agenzia di viaggi *travel agency*
amare *to love, to like*
andare *to go*
andarsene *to go away*
aria *air*
asciugamano *hand-towel*
bagnino *lifeguard*
bagno *bathe; bath*
barca *boat*
benvenuto *welcome*
calmo *calm*
campagna *country-side*
cielo *sky*
costume da bagno (m) *bathing costume*
crema solare *suntan lotion*
di solito *usually*
diapositiva *slide, transparency*
dimenticare *to forget*
durante *during*
estero (all'...) *abroad*
estivo *summer, summery*
ferie *holidays (R)*
forte *strong*
foto (f) *photograph*
galleria *gallery*
giorno feriale *working day,week-day (R)*
giorno festivo *holiday (R)*
giro *trip*
gita *excursion; school trip*
gruppo *group*
guida *guide*
in macchina *by car*
insieme, (... a) *together, (... with)*
interessante *interesting*
intorno a *around*
lago *lake*
lontano da *far from*
luce (f) *light*
macchina fotografica *camera*
mare (m) *sea*
molto tempo *a long time*
mondo *world*
montagna *mountain*
monumento *monument*
mosso *rough*
neve (f) *snow*
occhiali da sole *sun-glasses (R)*
ombrellone (m) *beach umbrella*
ospitalità *hospitality*
passeggiata *stroll, walk*
pattinare *to skate*
piacere *to please*
pista *track, piste*
più *more*
pomeriggio *afternoon*
preferire *to prefer*
progetti *plans*
Pro loco (f) *'local tourist office'*
prossimo *next*
pullman (m) *coach*
qualche volta *sometimes*
quasi *almost*
quindici giorni *fortnight*
quindicina; (... di giorni) *about fifteen; (a fortnight)*
restare *to stay*
ricordarsi *to remember*
rullino/rollino *film (for camera) (R)*
sabbia *sand*
sagra *festival, feast (R)*
salute (f) *health*
sano *healthy*
sciare *to ski*
sedia a sdraio *deck-chair*
settimana *week*
sole (m) *sun*
spiaggia *beach*
splendere *to shine*
stagione (f) *season*
storico *historic*
sulla riva del mare *by the sea shore*
tempo *time, weather*
tramonto *sunset*

Vocabulary

turismo	*tourism*
turista (m/f)	*tourist*
vacanza	*holiday*
viaggiatore (m)	*traveller*
viaggio	*journey*
villaggio	*village*
visitare	*to visit*
volta	*time*
week-end (m)	*week-end*

Geographical items: *(R)*

Città (Cities):
Londra (London), Edimburgo (Edinburgh), Parigi (Paris), Bruxelles (Brussels), Strasburgo (Strasbourg), Roma (Rome), Milano (Milan), Torino (Turin), Venezia (Venice), Firenze (Florence) Genova (Genoa), Pisa, Napoli (Naples), ...

Fiumi (Rivers):
Po, Adige, Tevere (Tiber), Adda, Arno, ...

Montagne (Mountains):
le Alpi (Alps), gli Appennini (Appennines), ...

Vulcani (Volcanoes):
Vesuvio (Vesuvius), Stromboli, Vulcano, Etna.

Laghi (Lakes):
Garda, Maggiore, Como, ...

Mari (Seas):
il Ligure (Ligurian), il Tirreno (Tyrrhenian), lo Ionio (Ionian), l'Adriatico (Adriatic), il Mediterraneo (the Mediterranean).

Regioni (Regions):
[North] Valle d'Aosta, Piemonte (Piedmont), Lombardia (Lombardy), Trentino-Alto Adige, Friuli-Venezia Giulia, Veneto, Liguria, Emilia-Romagna; [Centre] Toscana (Tuscany), Marche (The Marches), Umbria, Lazio (Latium), Abruzzo, Molise; [South] Campania, Puglia (Apulia), Basilicata, Calabria; [Islands] Sicilia (Sicily), Sardegna (Sardinia).

Tourist information

(see also Accommodation, Free Time and Entertainment)

a partire da	*starting from*
albergo	*hotel*
andare	*to go*
avere il tempo	*to have time*
ballare	*to dance*
campeggiare	*to camp*
capolavoro	*masterpiece*
cartina geografica	*(small) map*
cercare	*to look for*
certamente	*certainly*
cinema (m)	*cinema*
città	*town, city*
classico	*classic*
comprare	*to buy*
concerto	*concert*
depliant (m)	*leaflet, brochure*
divertente	*amusing*
divertimenti	*amusements*
domandare	*to ask*
fare delle passeggiate	*to go for walks*
generalmente	*generally, usually*
giocare (a tennis ecc.)	*to play (tennis etc.)*
informare	*to inform*
informarsi	*to enquire (about) (R)*
interessarsi	*to be interested in*
moderno	*modern*
museo	*museum*
musica	*music*
negozio	*shop*
opera	*opera*
opuscolo	*booklet,brochure*
parco	*park*
pianta (della città)	*map (of the town)*
presto	*soon*
pubblicità	*advertisement, advertising*

regione (f)	*region, area*
ristorante (m)	*restaurant*
sempre	*always*
spettacolo	*show, performance*
sport (m)	*sport*
teatro	*theatre*
trascorrere	*to pass, to spend*
trovarsi	*to be*
ufficio informazioni	*information office*
volere	*to want*
zoo	*zoo*

Feste — *holidays*

25 aprile	*25th April (Liberation Day)*
Assunzione	*Assumption of the Virgin Mary (15th August)*
Capodanno	*New Year's Day*
Epifania/Befana	*Epiphany (6th January)*
Ferragosto	*Mid-August bank holiday(s)*
I maggio	*1st May (Labour Day)*
Immacolata Concezione	*Immaculate Conception (8th Dec.)*
Lunedì dell'Angelo/di Pasqua	*Easter Monday*
Natale	*Christmas*
Pasqua	*Easter*
Santo Stefano	*Boxing Day (26th December)*
Tutti i Santi/Ognissanti	*All Saints' Day (1st November)*

Abbreviations

A.A.C.S.T./A.S. Azienda Autonoma di Cura, Soggiorno e Turismo *Autonomous Tourist Office*

A.I.G. Associazione Italiana Alberghi per la Gioventù *Italian Youth Hostel Association*

A.P.T. Azienda di Promozione Turistica *Tourist Promotion Board.*

C.A.I. Club Alpino Italiano *Italian Alpine Club*

C.I.T. Compagnia Italiana del Turismo *Italian Tourist Bureau*

E.N.I.T Ente Nazionale Italiano per il Turismo *Italian State Tourist Office*

E.P.T. Ente Provinciale per il Turismo *Provincial Tourist Office*

F.I.C. Federazione Italiana del Campeggio e del Caravanning *Italian Federation of Camping ....*

I.A.T. Informazione e Accoglimento Turistico *Information and Tourist Reception*

s.l.m. sul livello del mare *above sea level*

T.C.I. Touring Club Italiano *Italian Touring Club*

ACCOMMODATION

General

(see also Hotel, Youth Hostel, Camping)

arrivare	*to arrive*
albergo	*hotel*
camera	*room*
caro	*expensive*
comodo	*comfortable*
data	*date*
grande	*large, big*
giorno	*day*
libero	*free*
locanda	*inn (R)*
lontano da	*far*
mandare	*to send*
mezza pensione	*half board (R)*
moderno	*modern*
notte (f)	*night*
partire	*to leave*
passare	*to pass, to spend*
pensione (... completa)	*board (full ...)*
piccolo	*small*
prima colazione	*breakfast*
posto	*place*
per	*for*
potere	*to be able*
presso	*care of, near*

Vocabulary

ringraziare	*to thank*
rispondere	*to reply*
scrivere	*to write*
servire	*to serve*
settimana	*week*
trovarsi	*to be*
vitto e alloggio	*board and lodging (R)*
volere	*to want, to wish*

Hotel

albergo	*hotel*
altro	*other*
apprezzare	*to appreciate*
ascensore (m)	*lift*
bagagli (m, pl.)	*luggage*
camera	*room*
... per due persone	*double ...*
... per una persona	*single ...*
... matrimoniale	*double ...*
... a due letti	*... with twin beds*
... a un letto	*... with a single bed*
... con (il) bagno	*... with a bath*
... con (la) doccia	*... with a shower*
chiamare	*to call (R)*
chiave (f)	*key*
ciascuno	*each*
completo	*full*
compreso, incluso	*inclusive*
conto	*bill, amount*
dettaglio	*detail*
di gran lusso	*luxurious*
direttore (m)	*manager*
direzione (la ...)	*direction, management*
doppia	*double (R)*
entrata	*entrance, hallway*
gabinetti	*toilets*
impiegato	*employee*
lamentarsi	*to complain*
leggero	*light*
lista	*list, menu*
lordo	*gross*
mille	*thousand*
molto	*much*
numero (uno, ecc.)	*number (one, etc.)*
ora	*hour, time*
ospitalità	*hospitality*
padrone (m)	*owner*
pagare	*to pay*
passaporto	*passport*
piano	*floor, storey*
pianterreno	*ground floor*
portare	*to carry, to bring, to take*
premere (il bottone)	*to press (the button) (R)*
prenotare, riservare	*to book, to reserve*
prezzo massimo	*maximum price*
prezzo minimo	*minimum price*
privato	*private*
qualcosa	*something*
quale	*which*
quando	*when*
quanto	*how much*
ricevuta	*receipt (R)*
riservare	*to reserve*
ristorante (m)	*restaurant*
rumore (m)	*noise*
scale	*stairs*
seminterrato	*basement (R)*
senza	*without*
servito	*served*
solamente	*only*
solo	*alone*
svegliare	*to wake (R)*
telefono	*telephone*
televisore (m)	*television set*
trovare	*to find*
uscita di sicurezza	*emergency exit (R)*
valigia	*suitcase*
vista	*view*
visto	*visa*

Youth Hostel (Ostello della Gioventù)

Affittare	*to rent*
aiutare	*to help*
aperto	*open*
bagno	*bathroom*
benvenuto	*welcome*
chiudere	*to close*
chiuso	*closed*
colazione (f)	*breakfast*
completo	*full (R)*
coperta	*blanket*
costare	*to cost*
cucina	*kitchen*
doccia	*shower*
dormire	*to sleep*

dormitorio *dormitory*
gabinetti *toilets*
giorno *day*
letto *bed*
mappa *map*
ospite (m/f) *guest*
pagare *to pay*
paio, (un ... di lenzuola) *pair, (a ... of sheets)*
pasto *meal*
pasto pronto *ready to eat meal*
pattumiera *dustbin*
per giorno (persona, notte) *per day (person, night)*
posta *mail*
pranzare *to have lunch*
prenotare *to book, to reserve*
quanto *how much*
sacco a pelo *sleeping bag*
sala giochi *games room, amusement arcade*
sala da pranzo *dining room*
salvo *except*
silenzio *silence*
singola *single*
soggiorno *stay; living room*
tariffa *price list, charge*
tutto l'anno *all year round*
ufficio *office*
vacanza *holiday*
volere *to want*

Camping

accettare *to accept*
acqua (non) potabile *(non) drinking water*
adulto *adult*
aiutare *to help*
albero *tree*
bicchiere (m) *beaker, glass*
borraccia *water bottle*
branda *camp bed*
bussola *compass*
caldo *hot*
campeggiare *to camp*
campeggiatore (m) *camper*
campeggio; (andare in ...) *camping site; (to go camping)*
cercare *to look for*
coltello *knife*
corda *cord, rope*
cucchiaio *spoon*
dispensa portatile *food box*
elettrico *electric*
fiammiferi *matches*
forchetta *fork*
fornello a spirito/gas *spirit /gas stove*
freddo *cold*
gabinetti *toilets*
griglia (alla ...) *grilled*
lampada a gas *gas lamp*
lavabo *wash basin*
lavare *to wash*
lavatrice (f) *washing machine*
mazzuolo *mallet*
municipale *municipal, of the town*
nodo *knot*
picchetto *tent-peg*
pila *battery; 'torch'*
posizione (f) *position, situation*
preparare *to prepare*
presa (di corrente) *socket*
pulito *clean*
regolamento *regulations (R)*
roulotte (f) *caravan*
sacco per i rifiuti *rubbish bag (R)*
seggiolino, (... pieghevole) *stool, (folding stool)*
settimana *week*
spina (elettrica) *(electric) plug*
sporco *dirty*
supplemento *supplement*
tavola pieghevole *folding table*
tenda *tent*
termos (m) *thermos flask*
terreno *ground*
torcia elettrica *(electric) torch*
veicolo *vehicle*
veranda *verandah*
zaino *ruck-sack*

Vocabulary

FOOD AND DRINK

General

aceto *vinegar*
acqua minerale *mineral water*
affatto *at all*
affumicato *smoked*
altrettanto *and the same to you*
anche *also*
antipasto (misto) *hors d'oeuvre (mixed)*
apparecchiare *to lay the table*
appetitoso *appetizing (R)*
aranciata *orangeade*
arrosto *roast*
augurare *to wish*
ben cotto *well cooked*
bene *well*
benvenuto *welcome*
bere *to drink*
bevanda *drink*
bibita *(soft) drink*
birra *beer*
biscotto *biscuit*
boccone (m) *bite, mouthful*
brindare *to toast (R)*
brioche (f) *'brioche', 'bun'*
brodo; (riso in ...) *broth; (rice soup)*
buon appetito *enjoy your meal*
buono *good, nice*
burro *butter*
caffellatte (m) *white coffee*
caffettiera *coffee pot, coffee-maker*
caffè (m) *coffee*
caldo *hot*
cannelloni *cannelloni*
cappuccino *cappuccino*
caramelle *sweets*
casa; (fatto in ....) *house; (home made)*
cattivo *bad*
cena *dinner; supper*
cenare *to dine*
chiedere *to ask for*
cibo *food*
cincin! *cheers!*
cioccolata *chocolate*
coca-cola *coca-cola*
colazione (prima ...) (f) *breakfast*
coltello *knife*
come *as, how*
compere *shopping*
crema *cream; custard*
crostata *tart (R)*
cucchiaino *teaspoon*
cucchiaio *spoon*
cuoco *cook*
delizioso *delicious*
detestare *to detest, to hate*
di solito *usually*
dolce, dessert (m) *sweet, dessert*
dozzina (mezza ...) *dozen (half ...)*
far colazione *to have breakfast; to have lunch*
fare *to make, to do*
fetta *slice*
filoncino *long loaf*
forchetta *fork*
formaggio *cheese*
forno; (al ...) *oven; baked*
freddo *cold*
fresco *fresh, cool*
frittata *omelet*
frittella *fritter (R)*
fritto *fried*
galletta *cracker, biscuit*
gassosa *fizzy lemonade (R)*
gelato *ice cream*
ghiacciato *frozen, ice-cold*
grazie *thank you*
gusto *taste*
lasagne (f, pl.) *lasagna*
latte (m) *milk*
limonata *lemonade*
liquore; (liquori) (m) *liqueur; liquor; (spirits)*
maccheroni *macaroni*
macedonia *fruit salad*
maionese (f) *mayonnaise*
mangiare *to eat*
marmellata *marmalade, jam*
Marsala *Marsala*
Martini (m) *Martini*
mensa *canteen, refectory (R)*
merenda *(afternoon) snack*
metà *half*
mi piace, (non ...) *I like, I don't like*

minestra	*soup*
minestrina	*thin soup, broth*
minestrone (m)	*minestrone, vegetable soup*
molto	*much, a lot of*
mozzarella	*'mozzarella'*
olio di semi	*vegetable oil*
ora	*now*
padella	*frying pan*
pagnotta	*round loaf*
pane (m)	*bread*
passare	*to purée, to strain*
pasta	*pasta; pastry*
pasticceria	*pastry shop, 'patisserie', cakes*
pasto	*meal*
patate fritte	*chips, French fries*
patatine	*potato crisps*
pentola	*pot*
per cortesia	*please*
pezzo	*piece, a bit*
piattino	*saucer*
piatto	*plate; dish*
piccante	*spicy, hot*
picnic (m)	*picnic*
pietanza	*course; dish*
pizza	*pizza*
pranzare	*to lunch*
preferire	*to prefer*
prendere	*to take, to have*
preparare	*to prepare, to make*
provare	*to try*
provvista	*supply, stock*
ravioli	*ravioli*
ricetta	*recipe*
riso	*rice*
salato	*salty, salt (adj)*
sale (m)	*salt*
salute (alla ...!)	*cheers! good health!*
sapore (m)	*flavour, taste*
spaghetti	*spaghetti*
specie di	*type of*
spremuta	*fresh fruit juice*
squisito	*exquisite, delicious*
succo di frutta	*fruit juice*
tagliare	*to cut*
tagliatelle	*tagliatelle*
tavola	*table*
tazza	*cup*
teiera	*teapot*
tè (m)	*tea*
tipico (piatto ...)	*typical dish*
torta	*cake*
uovo	*egg*
vaniglia	*vanilla*
vassoio	*tray (R)*
vermut (m)	*vermouth*
vino (bianco, rosso, rosè)	*wine (white, red, rosé)*
yoghurt (m)	*yoghurt*
zuccherato	*sweetened; sugared*
zucchero	*sugar*
zuppa inglese	*'trifle'*
zuppa	*soup*

Café, Restaurant and other Public Places

a puntino (cotto a ...)	*cooked to a turn*
accomodarsi	*to take a seat, to come in*
acqua	*water*
al dente	*'firm to the bite'*
ancora	*again, more*
apprezzare	*to appreciate*
approvare	*to approve*
aver fame, sete	*to be hungry, thirsty*
aver vergogna di	*to be ashamed of*
aver voglia di	*to feel like*
bar (m)	*bar, café; cocktail cabinet*
bicchiere (m)	*glass*
birra	*beer*
boccale (m)	*jug (R)*
bottiglia	*bottle*
caffè (m)	*coffee; coffee house, café, bar*
cameriere (m)	*waiter*
capocuoco	*chef (R)*
caraffa	*carafe, decanter*
carta; (... dei vini, alla ...)	*menu; (wine list, à la carte)*
club (m)	*club*
come	*how, as*
completamente	*completely*
complimentarsi	*to compliment, to congratulate*
complimenti!	*Well done! Congratulations!*
consigliare	*to recommend*
contento	*happy, satisfied*

Vocabulary

conto	*bill*
contorno	*vegetables, side dish*
coperto	*cover charge*
cornetto	*'croissant', 'cornetto'*
costare	*to cost*
cotoletta	*cutlet, chop*
cucina	*kitchen; cooking*
dare	*to give*
desiderare	*to want, to wish*
dove	*where*
eccellente	*excellent*
errore (m)	*error, mistake*
esattamente	*exactly, precisely*
espresso	*espresso (coffee)*
fa lo stesso	*it's the same*
fiasco	*flask*
frizzante	*fizzy, sparkling (R)*
gabinetto	*toilet*
ghiaccio	*ice*
giusto	*right, fair*
gradire	*to enjoy, to like*
griglia (alla ...)	*grilled (R)*
in più	*more, extra*
inammissibile	*inadmissible, intolerable*
incluso/compreso	*included*
insultare	*to insult*
interamente	*entirely, completely*
irritarsi	*to get angry, to get annoyed*
lamentarsi	*to complain*
lesso	*boiled meat (R)*
litro	*litre*
locale (m)	*place, premises*
malato	*ill*
male di stomaco	*stomach ache*
mancia	*tip*
menu/menù (m)	*menu*
mezzo	*half*
nessuno	*no-one, nobody, none*
netto	*net, clear*
offrire	*to offer*
ordinare	*to order*
ordine (m)	*order*
padrone (m)	*owner*
panino; (... imbottito)	*roll; (filled roll, sandwich)*
per piacere/favore	*please*
persona	*person*
piatto (del giorno)	*dish (of the day)*
pizzeria	*'pizzeria'*
poco cotto	*underdone*
portare	*to carry, to bring, to take*
posto	*place, seat*
prenotare	*to book*
primo (piatto)	*first (course)*
protestare	*to complain, to protest*
quale	*which, what*
quanto	*how much*
quarto, (un ... di vino)	*quarter, (a ... litre of wine)*
regionale	*regional, local*
ristorante (m)	*restaurant*
saporito	*tasty*
sbaglio	*mistake, error*
scegliere	*to choose*
scelta	*selection, choice*
scontrino	*receipt*
secondo (piatto)	*second (course)*
servire	*to serve*
servizio	*service, service charge*
signore, signora	*Sir, Madam*
soddisfatto	*satisfied, pleased*
solo	*only, alone*
speciale; (è ...)	*special; (it is delicious)*
specialità	*speciality*
specie, (una ... di ...)	*type, (a type/kind of ...)*
spumante (m)	*'sparkling wine'*
supplemento	*supplement, extra portion, extra charge*
tavola calda	*snack bar, hot lunch counter*
tavolo	*table*
telefono	*telephone*
tipo	*type, kind*
tovaglia	*table cloth*
tovagliolo	*napkin*
trattoria	*(small) restaurant, inn, 'trattoria'*
troppo cotto	*overdone*
trovare	*to find*
turistico (menù ...)	*fixed-price menu*
un po'	*a bit, a little*
vario, (varie volte)	*varied, various, (several times)*
vegetariano	*vegetarian*
vergognarsi	*to be ashamed*
voglio, (non ...)	*I want, (I don't ...)*
vorrei	*I'd like*

Fruit and vegetables

aglio	*garlic*
albicocca	*apricot*
ananas (m)	*pineapple*
anguria	*water melon (R)*
arancia	*orange*
banana	*banana*
carciofo	*artichoke*
carota	*carrot*
cavolfiore (m)	*cauliflower*
cavolo	*cabbage*
cetriolo	*cucumber*
ciliegia	*cherry*
cipolla	*onion*
fagioli	*beans*
fagiolini	*string beans, French beans*
fragola	*strawberry*
frutta	*fruit*
fungo	*mushroom*
insalata; (... mista/russa)	*salad, lettuce; (mixed/Russian salad)*
lampone (m)	*raspberry*
limone (m)	*lemon*
mela	*apple*
melanzana	*aubergine (R)*
melone (m)	*melon*
oliva	*olive*
patata	*potato*
pepe (m)	*pepper*
peperone; (... rosso/verde)	*pepper; (red/ green ...)*
pera	*pear*
pesca	*peach*
piselli	*peas*
pomodoro	*tomato*
pompelmo	*grapefruit (R)*
porro	*leek*
sedano	*celery*
uva (f, sing.)	*grapes*
verdura (f, sing.)	*vegetables, greens*
zucchino	*courgette*

Meat and Fish

agnello	*lamb*
aragosta	*lobster (R)*
baccalà (m)	*dried salted cod (R)*
bistecca, (... ai ferri)	*steak, (grilled ...)*
bollito	*boiled meat (R)*
capretto	*kid (R)*
coniglio	*rabbit (R)*
cozze	*mussels*
frittura di pesce	*mixed fried fish*
frutti di mare (m, pl.)	*seafood*
gamberetti grigi/rossi	*shrimps/prawns*
granchio	*crab (R)*
maiale (m)	*pork*
manzo	*beef*
merluzzo	*cod (R)*
montone (m)	*mutton*
mortadella	*'mortadella'*
ostrica	*oyster (R)*
pesce (m)	*fish*
pollo	*chicken*
prosciutto (crudo/cotto)	*ham (cured/cooked)*
salame (m)	*salami*
salmone (m)	*salmon*
sardina	*sardine*
scampi	*scampi*
sogliola	*sole*
tacchino	*turkey*
tonno	*tuna*
trota	*trout*
vitello	*veal*
vongola	*clam*

SHOPPING

General

(See also Food and Drink)

a buon mercato	*cheap*
a partire da	*starting from (R)*
abbastanza	*enough, rather*
accettare	*to accept*
agenzia di cambio	*Bureau de change*
aiutare	*to help*
altro	*other*
andare, (... a cercare)	*to go. (... and look for)*
aperto	*open*
aprire	*to open*
ascensore (m)	*lift*
assaggiare	*to taste (R)*

Vocabulary

assai/molto	*very*
assegno turistico	*travellers' cheque*
aumentare	*to increase*
aumento	*increase*
aver bisogno di	*to need*
avere	*to have*
banca	*bank*
banconota	*banknote*
barattolo; (... di latta)	*jar,pot; (tin)*
basta così, grazie	*that's enough, thank you*
biglietto da diecimila lire	*ten thousand lire note*
bilancio	*balance, budget*
borsa	*bag*
bottega/negozio	*shop*
bottiglia	*bottle*
busta	*envelope*
c'è, ci sono	*there is, there are*
cambiare	*to change*
cambio	*exchange*
caro	*dear, expensive*
carrello	*trolley*
carta da lettere	*writing paper*
carta di credito	*credit card*
carta	*paper*
cartolina (postale)	*postcard*
cassa	*cash desk*
cerino	*(waxed) match*
cestino	*basket*
che cosa?	*what?*
chilo	*kilogramme*
chiudere	*to close, to shut*
cliente (m/f)	*customer*
commerciante (m/f)	*trader, shopkeeper*
commesso	*shop-assistant*
compilare	*to compile, to fill in*
comprare	*to buy*
compreso	*included*
contare	*to count*
conto	*bill, account*
corto	*short*
cosa	*thing*
costare	*to cost*
costoso	*expensive, dear*
credito	*credit*
cristalleria	*crystal-ware*
da parte (mettere ...)	*to put aside*
dare	*to give*
deodorante (m)	*deodorant*
desidera?	*can I help you?*
desiderare	*to wish, to want*
differente	*different*
differenza	*difference*
disco	*disc, record*
dispiacere	*to dislike, to regret, to be sorry*
documento (di riconoscimento)	*document (identity ...)*
domandare	*to ask*
dozzina	*dozen*
è tutto?	*is that all?*
eccetto	*except*
errore (m)	*mistake*
esatto	*exact*
essere	*to be*
etto	*100 grammes*
fare la spesa	*to do the shopping*
farsi prestare	*to borrow*
ferie (f, pl.)	*holidays (R)*
fetta	*slice*
fiammifero	*match*
firmare	*to sign*
non funziona	*out of order*
garanzia	*guarantee*
giocattolo	*toy*
gioielleria	*jeweller's (shop)*
gioiello	*jewel*
giornale (m)	*newspaper*
gradire	*to appreciate; to like*
grande	*large; big*
gratuito	*free (of charge) (R)*
grazie	*thank you*
guadagnare	*to earn*
guida	*guide*
I.V.A	*Value Added Tax (R)*
importato	*imported (R)*
imposta	*tax; duty*
incluso	*included*
istruzioni; (... per l'uso)	*instructions; (directions for use)*
lamentarsi	*to complain*
largo	*large; broad*
latte (m)	*milk*
lavorare	*to work*
leggero	*light*
libretto d'assegni	*cheque book*

Vocabulary

libro	*book*
lira	*lira*
lista/elenco	*list*
lungo	*long*
magazzino	*store, shop*
mancare	*to lack*
matita	*pencil*
meglio	*better, best*
meno; (un po'...)	*less; (a bit ...)*
mercato	*market*
mese (m)	*month*
metà	*half*
mettere	*to put; to wear*
mezzo	*half*
migliore	*better, best*
milione (m)	*million*
mille	*thousand*
misura	*size*
moda	*fashion*
modello	*model*
modulo	*form*
molto	*much, a lot*
moneta	*coin*
mostrare	*to show*
naturale	*natural*
negoziante (m/f)	*shopkeeper*
normale	*normal*
nuovo	*new*
offrire	*to offer*
ombrello	*umbrella*
orologio	*watch*
pacchetto	*(small) packet, parcel*
pacco	*parcel*
pagamento	*payment*
pagare	*to pay*
paio	*pair*
parecchio	*quite a lot of*
passaporto	*passport*
penna	*pen*
per piacere	*please*
però	*but, however*
pesante	*heavy*
pezzo	*piece*
piacere	*to like*
piano, (primo ...)	*floor, (first ...)*
pianterreno	*ground floor*
piccolo	*small*
poco	*little; not much*
porcellana	*porcelain, china*
portare	*to carry; to wear*
povero	*poor*
preferire	*to prefer*
prego!	*don't mention it!, you are welcome!*
prendere	*to take*
prestare	*to lend*
prezzo, (... fisso)	*price, (fixed ...)*
primo	*first*
profumo	*perfume*
provare	*to try*
qualche	*some, a few*
qualcosa	*something*
quale	*which*
qualità	*quality*
quantità	*quantity*
quanto, (... fa?)	*how much, (... is it?)*
reclamo	*complaint*
regalo	*present*
reparto	*department (R)*
resto	*change*
ricco	*rich*
ricevere	*to receive*
ricevuta	*receipt*
ricordo	*souvenir*
riduzione (f)	*reduction*
rimborsare	*to pay back (R)*
rimborso	*refund*
ringraziare	*to thank*
risparmiare	*to save*
ritornare	*to return*
rivista	*magazine*
rotto	*broken*
rullino/rollino	*film (for camera)*
sacchetto	*(small) bag*
saldi	*sales*
sbagliato	*wrong, mistaken*
sbaglio	*mistake*
scaffale (m)	*shelf*
scala mobile	*escalator*
scatola	*box*
scelta	*choice, selection*
sconto	*discount*
seminterrato	*basement*
settimana	*week*
shampoo (m)	*shampoo*
soldi (m, pl.)	*money*

Vocabulary

sopra	*on, over, above*
sostituire	*to substitute, to change (R)*
sotto	*under*
spendere	*to spend*
spesa; (fare la ...)	*shopping; (to do the shopping)*
spiccioli (m, pl.)	*small money, change*
sport (m)	*sport*
sterlina	*pound (sterling)*
stesso	*same*
supplemento	*extra charge*
svendita	*(clearance) sale*
tabaccaio	*tobacconist*
tascabile; (dizionario ...)	*pocket; (... dictionary)*
tassa	*tax, duty*
tempo libero	*free time*
travellers' cheque (m)	*travellers' cheque*
troppo	*too, too much*
trovare	*to find*
trucco	*make-up*
tutto	*all*
ufficio	*office*
uso	*use*
va bene	*all right*
vale	*it is worth*
valore (m)	*value, price*
vendere	*to sell*
vendita (in ...)	*for sale*
vergognarsi	*to be ashamed*
vero	*real, genuine (R)*
vetrina	*shop window*
volere	*to want*
vorrei	*I'd like*

Shops

abbigliamento (negozio di ...)	*clothes shop*
alimentari (negozio di ...)	*grocer's (shop)*
cartoleria	*stationery (shop)*
centro commerciale	*shopping centre*
drogheria	*grocer's (shop)*
edicola	*newspaper kiosk (R)*
farmacia	*pharmacy; chemist's (shop)*
fioraio	*florist*
fruttivendolo	*greengrocer's (shop)*
gelateria	*ice-cream (shop)*
gioielleria	*jeweller's (shop)*
giornalaio	*newsagent*
grande magazzino	*department store*
latteria	*dairy*
lavanderia	*laundry*
lavasecco/lavanderia a secco	*dry-cleaner's (shop) (R)*
libreria	*bookshop*
macelleria	*butcher's (shop)*
mercato	*market*
panetteria/fornaio	*baker's (shop)*
parrucchiere (m)	*hairdresser*
pasticceria	*confectioner's (shop)*
pastificio	*pasta factory (R)*
pescheria	*fishmonger's (shop) (R)*
profumeria	*perfumer's shop*
rosticceria	*roast meat shop, 'rôtisserie'*
salumeria	*delicatessen (shop)*
supermercato	*supermarket*
tabaccheria	*tobacconist's (shop)*
tintoria	*dry-cleaner's (shop) (R)*

Clothes

abbigliamento; (un negozio d'...)	*clothes; (a ... shop)*
allargare (i pantaloni)	*to let out (the trousers) (R)*
allungare (il vestito)	*to lengthen (the dress) (R)*
bikini (m)	*bikini*
blusa/camicetta	*blouse*
calze	*socks, stockings*
calzini	*socks*
calzoni	*trousers*
camicia	*shirt*
cappello	*hat*
cappotto	*(over) coat*
cintura	*belt*
collant, (un paio di ...)	*tights, (a pair of ...)*
costume da bagno (m)	*bathing costume*
cravatta	*tie*
fazzoletto	*handkerchief*
giacca a vento	*wind cheater; anorak*
giacca	*jacket*
gonna	*skirt*

impermeabile (m) *raincoat*
jeans (m, pl.) *jeans*
maglia *jersey*
pantaloni, (paio di ...) *trousers, (pair of ...)*
pigiama (m) *pyjamas*
pullover (m) *pullover*
sandali *sandals*
scarpa *shoe*
soprabito *overcoat*
stivale (m) *boot*
stoffa *cloth, material*
strappato (un vestito ....) *a torn dress*
stretto *tight*
stringere (la giacca) *to take in (the jacket) (R)*
taglia *size*
tasca *pocket (R)*
vestiti/abiti *clothes*
vestito *suit, dress*

Weights and measurements

abbastanza *enough*
leggero *light*
mezzo *half*
pesante *heavy*
pesare *to weigh*
peso, (...netto) *weight, (net ...)*

cg **centigrammo** *centigramme*
g grammo *gramme*
hg **ettogrammo** *hectogramme*
kg chilogrammo *kilogramme*
q quintale *quintal, 100 kg*
t **tonnellata** *tonne , 1,000 kg*

ml **millilitro** *millilitre*
cl **centilitro** *centilitre*
l litro *litre*

mm **millimetro** *millimetre*
cm centimetro *centimetre*
m metro *metre*
km chilometro *kilometre*

Materials

argento *silver*
carta *paper*
cotone (m) *cotton*
ferro *iron*
lana *wool*
legno *wood*
metallo *metal*
nailon *nylon*
oro *gold*
pelle (f) *leather*
plastica *plastic*
seta *silk*
stoffa *cloth, material*
velluto *velvet*
vetro *glass*

Colours

arancione *orange*
azzurro *azure, light blue*
bianco *white*
celeste *light blue*
chiaro *light*
colore *colour*
giallo *yellow*
grigio *grey*
marrone *brown*
nero *black*
rosa *pink*
rosso *red*
scuro *dark*
verde *green*
viola *violet*

SERVICES

Post Office & Telephone

all'estero *abroad*
ascoltare *to listen*
attimo *moment*
bene *well*
bolletta *bill (R)*
buca/cassetta delle lettere *letter box*
busta *envelope*

Vocabulary

cabina (telefonica) *telephone box (R)*
carta telefonica *phone-card*
cartolina (postale) *postcard*
centralino *telephone exchange (R)*
centralinista (m/f) *operator (R)*
chi parla? *who is speaking?*
chiamare *to call*
chiamata telefonica *telephone call*
corrispondenza *correspondence, mail*
da parte di *on behalf of*
destinatario *addressee (R)*
elenco telefonico *telephone directory (R)*
fare il numero *to dial the number*
fare uno sbaglio *to make a mistake*
fermo posta *poste restante*
fessura *slot*
foglio *page, sheet*
fragile *fragile (R)*
francobollo *stamp*
fuori servizio *out of service (R)*
gettone (m) *(telephone) token*
guasto *out of order*
impostare/imbucare *to post*
indirizzo *address*
interno *extension*
introdurre *to insert (R)*
l'altro ieri *the day before yesterday*
lettera *letter*
levata *collection (R)*
libero *free*
male *bad*
mandare *to send*
mittente (m/f) *sender (R)*
modulo *form*
moneta *coin*
non funziona *does not work*
numero *number*
occupato *engaged*
pacchetto (postale) *(small) parcel*
pacco *parcel*
Pagine Gialle *Yellow Pages*
parlare *to talk*
posta *mail*
posta aerea *air mail*
Posta Centrale *General Post Office*
postino/portalettere *postman (R)*
prefisso *area code (telephone)*
pronto! *hallo!*
qua, qui *here*
quando *when*
quanto costa? *how much is it?*
quanto *how much*
raccomandata, (fare un ...) *registered letter, (to send a ...)*
restituzione (delle monete) *returned (coins) (R)*
riagganciare (il ricevitore) *to hang up (R)*
ricevere *to receive*
richiamare *to call back (R)*
riempire/compilare *to fill in*
Sali e Tabacchi *tobacconist's (shop)*
segnale (m) *signal*
segreteria telefonica *answerphone (R)*
sentire *to hear*
sganciare *to lift up the receiver (R)*
spedire *to send*
suonare *to ring*
tabaccheria *tobacconist's (shop)*
tariffa (postale) *rates (postal), postage*
telefonare *to telephone*
telefono *telephone*
telegramma (m) *telegram*
ufficio postale *post office*
urbana/interurbana (telefonata ...) *local/long distance call (R)*
urgente *urgent*
vaglia (m) *postal order (R)*

Abbreviations

all. Allegato *Enclosed*
C.A.P. Codice di Avviamento Postale *Post code*
c.a. Corrente anno. *Of this year*
c.c.p. Conto Corrente Postale *Current Postal Account*
c/o Presso *Care of*
c.m. Corrente mese *Of this month*
C.P. Casella Postale *Post Office Box*
Ns; n/ Nostro *Our*
P.T. Poste e Telegrafi *Post and Telegraph*
PP.TT. Poste e Telecomunicazioni *Post & Telecommunications*
S.I.P. Società Italiana per l'Esercizio Telefonico *Italian Telephone Service*

V., V/ Vostro *Your*
Vs.; Vs/ Vostra lettera *Your letter*

c.so Corso *Main Street, Avenue*
P.za Piazza *Square*
Prov. Provincia *Province*
V.le Viale *Avenue*
V. Via *Street, Road*

Sig. Signore *Mr.*
Sig.ra Signora *Mrs.*
Sig.na Signorina *Miss*
Egr. Sig. Egregio Signore *Dear Sir*
Gent. Sig.ra. Gentile Signora *Dear Mrs.*
Dott. Dottore *Dr.*
Dott.ssa Dottoressa *Dr.*
Mitt. Mittente *Sender*
Prof. Professore *Professor, Teacher*
Prof.ssa. Professor *Teacher*

Bank or Exchange Office

accettare *to accept*
agenzia di cambio *exchange bureau*
assegno (bancario) *cheque (R)*
banca *bank*
banconota *banknote*
biglietto da diecimila lire *ten thousand lire note*
cambiare *to change*
cambio (corso del ...) *exchange, rate of exchange*
carta assegni *cheque card*
carta di credito *credit card*
cassa *cash desk, till*
cassa continua *night safe*
Cassa di Risparmio *(Savings) Bank (R)*
commissione (f) *commission*
conto corrente *current account*
denaro *money*
documento di riconoscimento *proof of identity*
firmare *to sign*
girare *to endorse*
interesse (m) *interest*
istituto di credito *bank (R)*
libretto di assegni *cheque book*
lira *lira*
modulo *form*
moneta *coin (R)*
passaporto *passport*
per cento *per cent*
prestito *loan*
ritirare *to withdraw*
saldo *settlement, balance (R)*
soldi (m, pl.) *money*
spiccioli (m, pl.) *small change*
sportello; (... automatico) *counter; (cash point)*
sterlina *pound (sterling) (R)*
travellers' cheque *travellers' cheque (R)*
ufficio di cambio *bureau de change*
valore *value*
valuta *currency (R)*

Abbreviations

c/c Conto Corrente. *Current Account*
C.E.E. Comunità Economica Europea *E.E.C. European Economic Community*
I.C.E. Istituto per il Commercio Estero *Foreign Trade Institute*
I.V.A. Imposta sul Valore Aggiunto *Value Added Tax (V.A.T.)*
S.p.A. Società per Azioni *Joint-stock company*
S.r.l. Società a responsabilità limitata *Limited Company (Ltd)*
L.it Lire italiane *Italian Lire*
L.st. Lire sterline *Pound (sterling)*

Lost Property

accusare *to accuse*
argento *silver*
arrabbiato *angry*
bianco *white*
bicicletta *bicycle*
bisogna *need, it is necessary*
borsa, (borsetta) *bag, (hand-bag)*
borsellino *purse*
braccialetto *bracelet*
carta d'identità *identity card*
cercare *to look for*
certo *certain*

Vocabulary

chiaro *clear, light*
chiave (f) *key*
cinepresa *cine-camera*
cognome (m) *surname*
collana *necklace*
colore (m) *colour*
come *as, like*
consolato *consulate*
contento *pleased*
dappertutto *everywhere*
data *date*
dentro *inside*
descritto *described*
descrizione (f) *description*
di sopra *upstairs (R)*
di sotto *downstairs (R)*
dimenticare *to forget*
Dio mio! *my God!*
dispiaciuto *sorry; annoyed*
diverso *different*
documenti (personali) *(identification) papers*
dopo *after*
dove *where*
dovere *duty, to have to*
dubitare *to doubt*
fino a *as far as, until*
firmare *to sign*
flash (m) *flash (light)*
forma *shape*
formidabile *formidable*
fortunato *lucky, fortunate*
furioso *furious*
furto *theft*
grande *big, large*
ieri, (l'altro ...) *yesterday, (the day before ...)*
impossibile *impossible*
ladro; (al ...!) *burglar, pickpocket; (stop thief!)*
largo *large*
lasciare *to leave*
libretto degli assegni *cheque book*
lungo *long*
macchina fotografica *camera*
marca *make*
mattino/mattina *morning*
medio *medium, average*
metallo *metal*
misura *size*
modulo *form*
moto (f) *motor-bike*
nero *black*
nessuno *no-one*
nuovo di zecca *brand new (R)*
nuovo *new*
oggi *today*
ombrello *umbrella*
oro *gold*
orologio *watch*
ovunque *everywhere*
passaporto *passport*
peccato (che ...!) *what a pity!*
pelle (f) *leather*
perdere *to lose*
pieno *full*
plastica *plastic*
pomeriggio *afternoon*
portafoglio *wallet*
possibile *possible*
prima *before*
provare *to try*
quando *when*
quello *that (one)*
questo *this (one)*
restituire *to give back*
rettangolare *rectangular*
ricompensa *reward*
riconoscere *to recognise*
ricordarsi *to remember*
ritrovare *to find*
rotondo *round*
rubare *to steal*
sapere *to know*
scoprire *to discover*
scuro *dark*
sfortunato *unfortunate, unlucky*
simile *similar, like*
sorprendersi *to be surprised*
statura *height*
stretto *narrow*
tasca *pocket*
trovare *to find*
ufficio oggetti smarriti *lost property office*
uguale *equal; like*
valigia *suit case*
vecchio *old*
vuoto *empty*

zaino *ruck-sack*

Having things repaired or cleaned

accettare *to accept*
aggiustare *to mend*
ago *needle (R)*
auto-stop (fare l'...) *to hitch-hike*
autorimessa *garage*
batteria *battery*
bene *well*
bisogna *it is necessary*
bottone (m) *button*
buco *hole*
cadere *to fall*
calzolaio *cobbler, shoe-repair shop*
cambiare *to change*
camminare *to walk*
capace *able*
cattivo *bad*
controllare/verificare *to check*
cucire *to sew*
dispiaciuto *displeased, sorry*
domani *tomorrow*
dopodomani *the day after tomorrow*
dovere *duty, to have to*
duro *hard*
elettricista (m) *electrician*
fare *to make, to do*
filo *cotton thread (R)*
fissare *to fix*
flash (m) *flash (light)*
freno *brake*
funzionare *to work*
garantire *to guarantee (R)*
gentile *kind*
guastarsi *to break, to fail*
guasto *out of order; breakdown*
idraulico *plumber*
impossibile *impossible*
imprestare/prestare *to lend*
in questo caso *in this case*
iniziare *to begin*
investire *to collide with*
lavaggio; (... automatico/a mano) *washing; (automatic/ hand car wash) (R)*
lavanderia (automatica) *launderette*
lavatura a secco *dry cleaning*
lavandino *sink*
lavare *to wash*
lavatrice (f) *washing machine*
mamma mia! *goodness gracious!*
marca *make (R)*
marce *gears*
meccanico *mechanic*
motore (m) *engine*
naturalmente *of course*
non ne vale la pena *it is not worth it*
nonostante *in spite of*
perdita *leak*
possibile *possible*
prego! *don't mention it!*
prendere in prestito *to borrow*
promettere *to promise*
pronto *ready*
proporre *to propose*
provare *to try*
pulire *to clean*
pulito *clean*
quanto tempo *how long*
raccomandare *to recommend*
radiatore (m) *radiator*
reclamare *to complain*
rendere *to give back, to return*
ricambio; (pezzo di ...) *replacement; (spare part)*
ricevuta *receipt*
rifiutare *to refuse*
rimborsare *to refund*
ringraziare *to thank*
riparare *to repair*
ritornare *to return*
rompersi *to break*
rotto *broken*
rumore (m) *noise*
ruota di scorta *spare wheel (R)*
scoppiato *burst*
soddisfatto *satisfied*
sporco *dirty*
stato *state, condition*
strano *strange*
suggerire *to suggest*
svendita *sale*
tra due ore *in two hours*
velocità *speed*
vergognarsi *to be ashamed*

Vocabulary

HEALTH AND WELFARE

General

aiuto	*help*
aver mal di denti	*to have a tooth ache*
gola	*sore throat*
schiena	*back ache*
stomaco	*stomach ache*
testa	*head ache*
ammalarsi	*to fall ill*
ammalato	*ill*
andare (a letto)	*to go (to bed)*
asciugamano	*hand/face towel*
asciugarsi	*to dry (oneself)*
bene	*well*
bocca	*mouth*
braccio	*arm*
caldo	*hot, warm*
capelli (m, pl.)	*hair*
caviglia	*ankle*
coricarsi	*to go to bed; to lie down*
cuore (m)	*heart*
dentifricio	*tooth-paste*
dito	*finger*
dormire	*to sleep*
fame (f)	*hunger*
fare il bagno	*to have a bath*
fare la doccia	*to have a shower*
farsi la barba	*to shave*
fegato	*liver*
forse	*perhaps*
fragile	*fragile,weak*
freddo	*cold*
gamba	*leg*
ginocchio	*knee*
lavarsi	*to wash*
letto	*bed*
lingua	*tongue*
malato	*ill*
mano (f)	*hand*
normale	*normal*
occhio	*eye*
orecchio	*ear*
osso	*bone*
pelle (f)	*skin*
pericoloso	*dangerous*
piede (m)	*foot*
preoccupazione (f)	*worry, concern*
pulito	*clean*
rasoio	*razor*
rilassarsi	*to relax*
salute (f)	*health*
sangue (m)	*blood*
sapone (m)	*soap*
sciampo/shampoo	*shampoo*
sete (f)	*thirst*
spalla	*shoulder*
sporco	*dirty*
stanco	*tired*
stare meglio	*to be better*
va bene	*it is all right, fine*

Illness and injury

ambulanza	*ambulance*
ambulatorio	*consulting room, surgery*
annegare	*to drown*
ansioso	*anxious*
appuntamento	*appointment*
armadietto dei medicinali	*medicine cabinet*
aspirina	*aspirin*
assicurato	*insured*
assicurazione (f)	*insurance*
attacco	*fit, stroke, attack*
benda	*bandage*
bisogna	*it is necessary (R)*
bruciarsi la mano	*to burn one's hand*
cadere	*to fall*
cancro	*cancer*
cerotto (adesivo)	*(sticking) plaster*
clinica	*clinic*
colpo di sole	*sunstroke*
compressa	*tablet (R)*
consigliare	*to advise*
contro	*against*
cotone idrofilo	*cotton-wool (R)*
crisi (f, sing.)	*attack*
cucchiaiata	*spoonful*
dentista (m/f)	*dentist*
diarrea	*diarrhoea*
dieta	*diet*
dolore (m)	*pain*

dopo	*after*
dottore (m)	*doctor*
dovere	*duty, to have to*
è necessario	*it is necessary (R)*
essere ammesso	*to be admitted*
farmacia	*chemist's (shop)*
farmacista (m/f)	*chemist*
far male	*to hurt*
farsi male	*to hurt oneself*
fascia	*bandage*
fasciatura	*dressing, bandages*
febbre (f)	*fever, high temperature*
febbre da fieno	*hay fever*
ferito	*wounded*
fresco	*fresh*
giorno	*day*
grave	*serious*
gravemente	*gravely, seriously*
guarire	*to recover*
incendio	*fire*
indigestione (f)	*indigestion*
influenza	*infuenza*
ingessare	*to put in plaster*
isolamento	*isolation*
malattia	*illness*
mal di mare	*sea-sickness*
medico	*doctor*
medicamento	*medicament, medicine*
medicina	*medicine*
medicinale	*medicinal, medicine (R)*
meglio	*better*
molto tempo, a lungo	*long, a long while*
mordere	*to bite*
morire	*to die*
morto	*dead*
occhiali	*spectacles*
operazione (f)	*operation*
ora	*hour, now*
ospedale (m)	*hospital*
ottico	*optician, optical*
otturazione (f)	*filling*
ovatta	*cotton-wool*
pastiglia	*tablet*
paziente (m/f)	*patient*
piangere	*to cry*
pillola	*pill*
pomata	*ointment, cream*
preoccuparsi	*to worry, to be troubled*
prima	*before, first*
problema (m)	*problem*
pronto soccorso	*first aid*
puntura	*injection (R)*
qualche cosa	*something*
raffreddato (essere ...)	*to have a cold*
ricetta	*prescription*
rimedio	*remedy*
riposarsi	*to rest*
rompersi il braccio (ecc.)	*to break one's arm (etc.)*
salute (f)	*health*
sanguinare	*to bleed*
sciroppo	*syrup, mixture*
sentirsi	*to feel*
sofferente	*suffering, ill*
soffrire	*to suffer*
stare male	*to feel ill*
stare peggio	*to be worse*
tagliarsi	*to cut*
tosse (f)	*cough*
tubetto	*tube*
vedere	*to see*
viso	*face*
vivo	*alive*
voce (f)	*voice*
volere	*to want*
vomitare	*to vomit*

Accident

(moto) ciclista	*(motor) cyclist*
accusare	*to accuse*
aiutare	*to help*
all'improvviso	*suddenly*
ambulanza	*ambulance*
amico	*friend*
arrabbiarsi	*to get angry*
aspettare	*to wait*
assicurato	*insured*
attenzione!	*Look out!, Caution!*
attraversare	*to cross*
autobus (m)	*bus*
autocarro	*lorry*
avere il diritto	*to have the right*
avere la precedenza	*to have the right of way (R)*
avere paura	*to be afraid*

Vocabulary

avvertire	*to warn, to inform*
bagnato	*wet*
barella	*stretcher*
britannico	*British*
bruciare	*to burn*
cabina telefonica	*telephone box*
cadere	*to fall*
camminare	*to walk*
carabiniere (m)	*'carabiniere', 'policeman'*
carreggiata	*carriage way*
carta d'identità	*identity card*
caserma dei carabinieri	*police station ('carabinieri')*
certo	*certainly*
chiamare	*to call*
circolare	*to drive round, to keep moving*
codice (stradale) (m)	*(highway) code (R)*
collisione (f)	*collision*
colpa	*fault*
commissariato	*police station*
condurre	*to drive, to lead*
conduttore (m)	*driver*
consolato	*consulate*
correre	*to run, to speed*
corriera	*coach*
d'accordo	*agreed*
danno	*damage*
dichiarare	*to declare*
dichiarazione (f)	*statement (R)*
domanda	*question*
dopo	*after*
eppure	*and yet (R)*
falso	*false*
fare attenzione	*to be careful*
fare	*to do, to make*
ferito	*wounded*
fermarsi	*to stop*
fortunatamente	*luckily*
fuoco, (al ...!)	*fire, (fire!)*
girare	*to turn*
grave	*serious*
gridare	*to shout*
guardare	*to watch*
guidatore (m)	*driver*
immediatamente	*immediately*
improvvisamente	*suddenly*
incidente (m)	*accident*
indirizzo	*address*
informare	*to inform*
investire	*to collide with, to run over*
investito	*hit*
là	*there*
macchina	*car*
mamma mia!	*dear me!, my goodness!*
marca	*make (R)*
marciapiede (m)	*pavement*
medico	*doctor*
mettere	*to put*
mi scusi	*excuse me; I'm sorry*
morto	*dead*
multa	*fine*
nome (m)	*name*
numero	*number*
ospedale (m)	*hospital*
pagare	*to pay*
passante (m/f)	*passer-by*
passare	*to pass*
patente (f)	*driving licence*
Pazienza!/Non importa!	*Never mind!*
pedone (m)	*pedestrian*
pericolo	*danger*
permesso	*permission*
piangere	*to cry*
piano	*gently, carefully*
più tardi	*later*
polizia	*police*
polizza d'assicurazione	*insurance policy*
pompiere (m)	*fireman*
posto di polizia	*police station*
prego!	*don't mention it!*
presto!	*quick!*
problema (m)	*problem*
prossimo	*next*
protestare	*to protest*
purtroppo	*unfortunately*
quasi	*almost*
questura	*police headquarters*
qui, qua	*here*
rallentare	*to slow down (R)*
responsabile	*responsible*
riempire/compilare	*to fill in (R)*
riparare	*to repair (R)*
rischio	*risk*

rispettare	*to respect*
rovesciarsi	*to overturn*
sbrigarsi	*to hurry up*
scontro	*collision, crash*
scusare	*to excuse*
scusarsi	*to apologize*
semaforo	*traffic lights*
senso unico	*one way*
sicuro	*sure, safe*
slittare	*to slide*
sopralluogo	*on the spot investigation (R)*
sorpassare	*to overtake*
sorprendente	*surprising (R)*
sorpresa	*surprise*
spiacente	*sorry*
strada	*road*
subito	*immediately*
targa	*number plate*
telefonare	*to telephone*
testimone (m/f)	*witness (R)*
traversare	*to cross*
troppo presto	*too soon*
tutti	*all*
uccidere	*to kill*
urgente	*urgent*
urto	*collision, impact*
vedere	*to see*
veicolo	*vehicle (R)*
vero	*true*
vigili del fuoco	*firemen*
volere	*to want*

Abbreviations

C.R.I. Croce Rossa Italiana *Italian Red Cross*

I.N.P.S. Istituto Nazionale di Previdenza Sociale *National Institute of Social Insurance*

S.P.E. Soccorso Pubblico d'Emergenza *Public Emergency Assistance*

U.S.L. Unità Sanitaria Locale *Local Health Unit*

FREE TIME AND ENTERTAINMENT

andare a cavallo	*to go on horseback, to ride*
andare al mare	*to go to the seaside*
andare in bicicletta	*to cycle*
andare in campagna	*to go to the countryside*
andare in montagna	*to go to the mountains*
annoiarsi	*to get bored*
arte (f)	*art*
atletica	*athletics*
attore (m)	*actor*
ballare	*to dance*
biblioteca	*library*
biglietto	*ticket*
calcio (gioco del ...)	*football*
camminare	*to walk*
campeggio	*camping site*
campionato	*championship*
canna da pesca	*fishing rod*
cantante (m/f)	*singer*
cantare	*to sing*
canzone (f)	*song*
cartoni animati	*cartoons*
centro giovanile	*youth club*
chitarra	*guitar*
ciclismo	*cycling*
cinema (m)	*cinema*
circo	*circus*
collezionare	*to collect*
collezione (f)	*collection*
computer (m)	*computer*
concerto	*concert*
concorso	*competition*
dama	*draughts*
discoteca	*discotheque*
elefante (m)	*elephant*
elettronica	*electronics*
essere di moda	*to be in fashion*
fare la coda/la fila	*to queue*
fare un gol	*to score a goal*
fotografia	*photography*
gara	*competition*
giocare a pallone (bocce, carte)	*to play football (bowls, cards)*
giocare a dama	*to play draughts*
giocare a scacchi	*to play chess*
giornale (m)	*newspaper*

Vocabulary

gita	*excursion, trip*
gruppo	*group*
guida	*guide*
leggere	*to read*
leone (m)	*lion*
moda	*fashion*
museo	*museum*
musica classica	*classical music*
musica popolare	*folk music*
nuotare	*to swim*
nuoto	*swimming*
opera	*opera*
orchestra	*orchestra*
orso	*bear*
pallanuoto	*water-polo*
pallacanestro	*basket-ball*
pattini a rotelle	*roller-skates*
pattinare su ghiaccio	*to ice-skate*
pescare	*to fish*
pianoforte (m)	*piano*
piscina	*swimming pool*
pista	*rink, (ski) run, (dance) floor*
preferire	*to prefer*
programma (m)	*programme*
pugilato	*boxing*
quotidiano	*daily*
radio (f)	*radio*
ridere	*to laugh*
riunione (f)	*meeting*
rivista	*magazine*
scacchi	*chess*
sci	*skiing*
sciare	*to ski*
scimmia	*monkey*
sport acquatico	*water sport*
strumento musicale	*musical instrument*
svago	*amusement, recreation, hobby*
teatro	*theatre*
televisione (f)	*television*
tennis (m)	*tennis*
tigre (f)	*tiger*
tuffarsi	*to dive*
video	*video*
zoo	*zoo*

RELATIONS WITH OTHERS

General

amare	*to love, to like*
amico	*friend*
anche	*also*
andare	*to go*
apprezzare	*to appreciate*
ascoltare	*to listen to*
attività	*activity*
avere	*to have*
ballare	*to dance*
capire	*to understand*
capirsi	*to understand each other*
centro giovanile	*youth club*
circolo	*club*
club (m)	*club*
conoscere	*to know; to meet*
contento	*happy, glad*
di solito	*usually*
disco	*disc, record*
discutere	*to discuss*
divertirsi	*to enjoy oneself*
essere	*to be*
fare	*to make, to do*
frequentare	*to attend*
giocare	*to play*
giovane	*young*
gioventù (f)	*youth*
gruppo	*group*
interessarsi di	*to be interested in*
membro	*member*
musica	*music*
occuparsi di	*to occupy oneself with, to deal with*
parlare	*to talk, to speak*
partecipare	*to take part in*
passare	*to pass, to spend*
passatempo	*pastime, hobby*
pensare	*to think*
quando	*when*
quata (d'iscrizione)	*entrance fee (R)*
ringraziare	*to thank*
riunione (f)	*meeting*
sempre	*always*
socio	*member*
spesso	*often*

tessera (d'iscrizione) *membership card*
verità *truth*

Making Acquaintances

accompagnare *to accompany*
arrivederci *goodbye*
assicurare *to assure, ensure*
augurare *to wish*
bene *well*
benvenuto *welcome*
buon anno *happy new year*
buongiorno *good morning*
buon viaggio *have a good journey*
buona fortuna *good luck*
buonanotte *good night*
buonasera *good evening*
collega (m/f) *colleague*
come stai?, come sta? (formal) *how are you?*
congratulazioni *congratulations*
conoscente (m/f) *acquaintance*
conoscenza *acquaintance*
finalmente *at last*
gente (f, sing.) *people*
Inghilterra *England*
inglese *English*
insopportabile *unbearable*
Italia *Italy*
italiano *Italian*
lettera *letter*
persona *person*
piacere! *pleased to meet you!*
presentare *to introduce*
ricambiare *to return, to reciprocate*
vedersi *to meet*

Arranging a meeting or an activity

a che ora? *at what time?*
a destra *on the right*
a domani *see you tomorrow*
accettare *to accept*
accompagnare *to accompany*
allora *then*
appuntamento *appointment, date*
arrivare *to arrive*
aspettare *to wait*
avere il tempo di *to have the time to*
bene *well*
certamente *of course, certainly*
cinema (m) *cinema*
con piacere *with pleasure*
costare *to cost*
d'accordo *agreed*
decidere *to decide*
di buon'ora *early*
di nuovo *again*
dimenticare *to forget*
dipende da *it depends on*
domandare *to ask*
domani *tomorrow*
dove *where*
dovere *to have to, duty*
è necessario *it is necessary*
esagerare *to exaggerate, to go too far*
forse *perhaps, may be*
gentile *kind*
idea *idea*
impossibile *impossible*
in ritardo *late*
incontrare *to meet*
incontrarsi ancora *to meet again*
insieme *together*
intenzione (f) *intention*
invitare *to invite*
invito *invitation*
libero *free*
mattina *morning*
mi dispiace di... *I regret that..*
momento *moment*
naturalmente *of course, naturally*
non vale la pena *it's not worth it*
non vedere l'ora di *to look forward to*
offrire *to offer*
parco *park*
passeggiata *walk*
peccato (che ...!) *what a pity!*
perché *why, because*
permesso *permission*
piacere *to like*
pomeriggio *afternoon*
possibile *possible*
preferire *to prefer*
prima di *before*
promettere *to promise*

Vocabulary

proporre	*to propose*
prossimo	*next*
quasi	*almost*
ragione (f)	*reason*
rifiutare	*to refuse, to turn down*
sapere	*to know, to be able to*
scusarsi	*to apologize*
sera/serata	*evening*
settimana	*week*
sorpresa	*surprise*
suggerire	*to suggest*
supporre	*to suppose, to think*
televisione (f)	*television*
unico	*only, unique*
uscire	*to leave, to go out*
vedere	*to see*
vedersi	*to see, to meet*
venire	*to come*
visto che	*considering that*
volentieri	*willingly, gladly*
volere	*to want, to wish*

Current affairs

ambiente (m)	*environment*
attualità	*current affairs*
aumento	*increase, rise*
carestia	*famine*
comunista	*communist*
criminalità	*crime*
crisi	*crisis*
debito	*debt*
democratico	*democratic*
destra (di ...)	*right-wing*
dibattere	*to debate*
disarmo	*disarmament (R)*
discutere	*to discuss*
disoccupato	*unemployed*
ecologia	*ecology*
elezione (f)	*election*
emigrazione (f)	*emigration*
energia	*energy, power*
giustizia	*justice*
governo	*government*
guerra	*war*
guerriglia	*guerilla warfare*
inchiesta	*investigation, inquiry (R)*
inflazione (f)	*inflation*
inquinamento	*pollution*
libertà	*freedom (R)*
litigare	*to argue*
manifestazione (f)	*demonstration*
ministro	*minister*
nazionalismo	*nationalism (R)*
ottimista	*optimist*
pace (f)	*peace*
parlamento	*parliament*
partito	*party*
pessimista	*pessimist*
politica	*politics, policy*
povertà	*poverty (R)*
presidente (m)	*president*
presidente del consiglio	*prime minister*
problema (m)	*problem, issue*
reddito	*income*
ricchezza	*wealth (R)*
sciopero	*strike*
sequestrare	*to kidnap, to confiscate*
siccità	*drought*
sindacato	*trade union*
sinistra (di ...)	*left-wing*
socialista	*socialist*
sviluppo	*development*
tassa, imposta	*tax*
terrorismo	*terrorism*
terzo mondo	*third world*
violenza	*violence*
votare	*to vote*

Major Political Parties & Trade Unions

D.C. Democrazia Cristiana *Christian Democrat Party*

M.S.I.-D.N. Movimento Sociale Italiano - Destra Nazionale *Italian Social Party - National Right*

P.C.I. Partito Comunista Italiano *Italian Communist Party*

P.L.I. Partito Liberale Italiano *Italian Liberal Party*

P.R. Partito Radicale *Radical Party*

P.R.I. Partito Repubblicano Italiano *Italian Republican Party*

P.S.DI. Partito Socialista Democratico Italiano *Italian Socialist Democrat Party*
P.S.I Partito Socialista Italiano *Italian Socialist Party*

C.G.I.L Confederazione Generale Italiana del Lavoro *General Federation of Italian Trade Unions*
C.I.S.L. Confederazione Italiana Sindacati Lavoratori *Italian Federation of Trade Unions*
U.I.L. Unione Italiana del Lavoro *Italian Labour Union*

EDUCATION AND FUTURE CAREER

(see also Occupations)

abbastanza — *enough, quite, fairly*
abituarsi a — *to be accustomed to, to get used to*
abitudine (f) — *habit, custom*
accompagnare a scuola — *to take to school*
adesso — *now*
affari — *business*
agricoltore (m) — *farmer*
alunno — *pupil*
ambizione (f) — *ambition*
anche — *also, too*
anno — *year*
annoiarsi — *to be bored*
apprendere — *to learn*
arredatore (m) — *interior designer (R)*
arrivare — *to arrive*
artigiano — *craftsman*
ascoltare — *to listen to*
asilo (infantile) — *nursery*
assente — *absent*
attenzione; (ascoltare con ...) — *attention, to listen carefully*
attualmente — *at present, at the moment (R)*
aula — *classroom*
aver ragione/torto — *to be right/wrong*
avvenire (m) — *future*
ballo — *dance, ball*
banca — *bank*
banco — *desk*
bene — *well*
biblioteca — *library*
bisogna — *it is necessary that*
bocciare — *to fail*
borsa di studio — *grant, scholarship*
bravo (in) — *good (at)*
buono — *good*
calcio — *football*
campionato — *championship*
campione (m) — *champion*
capire — *to understand*
capitano — *captain*
carriera — *career*
carta, (un foglio di ...) — *paper, (a sheet of ...)*
cattedra — *teacher's desk*
certificato — *certificate*
chiedere — *to ask*
circolo — *club*
classe (f) — *class*
collegio — *boarding school*
colto — *well-educated*
come — *like, as, how*
cominciare — *to begin, to start*
commerciale — *commercial*
commercio — *commerce, trade*
compito — *homework*
condotta — *behaviour*
conoscere — *to know*
consigliare — *to advise, to recommend*
continuare — *to continue*
correggere — *to correct, to mark*
corretto — *correct*
corso; (... serale) — *course; (evening class)*
cortile (m) — *playground, courtyard (R)*
credere — *to believe*
cultura — *culture, education*
dare — *to give*
debole (in) — *weak (in)*
decoratore (m) — *decorator*
dentista (m/f) — *dentist*
detestare — *to detest, to hate*
difficile — *difficult*
difficoltà — *difficulty*
dipende da ... — *depends on*
diploma (...di maturità) (m) — *diploma, (school leaving certificate)*

Vocabulary

direttore (m)	*headmaster*
direttrice (f)	*headmistress*
disoccupato	*unemployed*
disoccupazione	*unemployment*
diventare/divenire	*to become*
divertente	*amusing, funny*
divertirsi	*to enjoy oneself*
dopo	*after*
dovere	*duty, to have to*
dubbio (senza ...)	*doubt (no ...)*
durare	*to last*
durata	*duration, length*
educazione (f)	*upbringing*
elementare; (scuola ...)	*elementary; (primary school)*
errore; (... d'ortografia) (m)	*mistake, error; (spelling mistake)*
esame (m)	*exam*
esempio	*example*
estero (all' ...)	*abroad*
età	*age*
fabbrica	*factory*
facile	*easy*
fare	*to make, to do*
finire	*to finish*
forse	*perhaps*
frase (f)	*sentence, phrase*
frequentare	*to attend*
futuro	*future*
gesso	*chalk*
ginnasio	*first two years of 'classical lycée'*
giocare	*to play*
gioco	*game*
giornata	*day*
gita	*trip, outing*
gomma	*rubber*
gruppo	*group*
guaio	*trouble, difficulty*
guardare	*to look*
imparare	*to learn*
impiegato	*employee*
impiego	*employment, job*
impossibile	*impossible*
inchiostro	*ink*
indicare	*to indicate, to show*
indovinare	*to guess*
infine	*at last, finally*
ingegnere (m)	*engineer*
insegnante (m/f)	*teacher*
insegnare	*to teach*
intelligente	*intelligent*
intendere	*to understand*
interessante	*interesting*
interessare	*to interest*
interessarsi di	*to be interested in*
intervallo	*break*
iscrizione (f)	*enrolment*
istruito	*educated, learned*
istruzione (f)	*education*
laboratorio	*laboratory, work shop*
lasciare	*to leave*
laurea	*degree*
laurearsi	*to graduate*
lavagna	*blackboard*
lavorare	*to work*
lavoro; (... manuale)	*work, job; (manual work)*
leggere	*to read*
lettura	*reading*
lezione (f)	*lesson*
libro	*book*
liceo, (... classico, scientifico)	*'liceo', (classical, scientific 'lycée')*
lingua	*language*
maestro	*(primary) teacher*
matita	*pencil*
media	*average*
mensa	*canteen*
molto	*much*
necessario	*necessary*
negozio	*shop*
noioso	*boring*
nuotare	*to swim*
nuoto	*swimming*
obbligatorio	*compulsory*
ogni	*every*
opinione (f)	*opinion*
ora	*hour, time*
orario	*timetable*
ottimo	*very good, excellent*
paga	*pay, wage*
pagina	*page*
palestra	*gymnasium*
palla	*ball*
pallone (m)	*foot-ball*
partita	*match, game*

Vocabulary

passatempo	*pastime, hobby*
perché	*why, because*
permesso	*permission*
permettere	*to permit, to allow*
personale (m)	*staff, personnel*
piacere	*pleasure; to like*
piscina	*swimming pool*
pittura	*painting, paint*
più	*more*
poco	*little, not much*
poesia	*poetry, poem*
poeta (m)	*poet*
poi	*then, later*
possibilità	*possibility*
posto; (...di lavoro)	*place, space; (job)*
preferire	*to prefer*
presente	*present*
preside (m/f)	*headmaster/mistress*
problema (m)	*problem, issue*
professione (f)	*profession, occupation*
professore (m)	*teacher, professor*
professoressa	*teacher, professor*
progresso	*progress*
promuovere	*to pass*
provare	*to try*
punire	*to punish*
punizione (f)	*punishment*
quaderno	*exercise book*
quando	*when*
quanto	*how much*
raccontare	*to tell*
racconto	*story*
restare	*to stay*
ricreazione (f)	*recreation, break (R)*
righello	*ruler*
ripetere	*to repeat*
rispondere	*to reply*
risultato	*result, answer*
ritardo	*late*
ritorno	*return*
romanzo	*novel*
salario	*salary, wage (R)*
sapere	*to know*
sbaglio	*mistake*
scadente	*unsatisfactory, poor quality (R)*
scambio	*exchange*
scegliere	*to choose*
scelta	*choice*
scientifico	*scientific*
sciocco	*silly*
scolaro	*pupil, school boy*
scoperta	*discovery*
scopo	*purpose, aim*
scoprire	*to discover, to find out*
scorretto	*incorrect*
scrivere	*to write*
scuola privata	*private school*
scuola pubblica/statale	*State school*
scuola media	*first three years of secondary school*
segretario	*secretary*
sera	*evening*
severo	*strict*
sforzarsi di	*to make an effort*
società	*society, club*
sodo	*hard*
sperare	*to hope*
spiegare	*to explain*
sport (m)	*sport*
stare	*to stay*
straniero	*foreigner, foreign*
strumento	*instrument*
studente (m), studentessa	*student*
studiare	*to study*
studio	*study*
studioso	*studious*
suonare	*to ring, to play*
tardi (più ...)	*later*
teatro	*theatre, drama*
tema (m)	*essay, composition*
tennis (m)	*tennis*
tradurre	*to translate*
traduzione (f)	*translation*
trovare	*to find*
tutto	*all*
ubbidire	*to obey*
uniforme	*uniform*
università	*university*
vacanza	*holiday*
vero	*true*
vincere	*to win*
vita	*life*
vocabolario	*vocabulary*
voglia; (aver ... di)	*wish; (to feel like)*
volere	*to want, to wish*

Vocabulary

voto, (aver voti belli/brutti) *mark (to have good/bad marks)*

Subjects

biologia *biology*
ceramica *pottery*
chimica *chemistry*
dattilografia *typing*
economia *economics*
educazione artistica *art*
educazione civica *civics*
educazione fisica *physical education*
educazione musicale *music*
educazione tecnica *technical education*
elettronica *electronics*
fisica *physics*
francese (m) *French*
geografia *geography*
greco *Greek*
inglese (m) *English*
italiano *Italian*
latino *Latin*
letteratura *literature*
lingue moderne *modern languages*
matematica *maths*
morale (f) *ethics*
musica *music*
ragioneria *accounting*
religione (f) *religious education*
scienze (f, pl.) *science*
scienze naturali *natural sciences*
scienze umane *human sciences*
sociologia *sociology*
spagnolo *Spanish*
stenografia *shorthand*
storia dell'arte *history of art*
storia *history*
teatro *drama*
tedesco *German*

VERB TABLE

INDICATIVE (INDICATIVO)

	ESSERE	AVERE	ABITARE	RIPETERE	PARTIRE
PRESENT					
(io)	sono	ho	abit**o**	ripet**o**	part**o**
(tu)	sei	hai	abit**i**	ripet**i**	part**i**
(lui, lei,Lei)	è	ha	abit**a**	ripet**e**	part**e**
(noi)	siamo	abbiamo	abit**iamo**	ripet**iamo**	part**iamo**
(voi)	siete	avete	abit**ate**	ripet**ete**	part**ite**
(loro)	sono	hanno	abit**ano**	ripet**ono**	part**ono**
PERFECT					
	sono stato/a	ho avuto	ho abit**ato**	ho ripet**uto**	sono part**ito/a**
	sei stato/a	hai avuto	hai abitato	hai ripetuto	sei partito/a
	è stato/a	ha avuto	ha abitato	ha ripetuto	è partito/a
	siamo stati/e	abbiamo avuto	abbiamo abitato	abbiamo ripetuto	siamo partiti/e
	siete stati/e	avete avuto	avete abitato	avete ripetuto	siete partiti/e
	sono stati/e	hanno avuto	hanno abitato	hanno ripetuto	sono partiti/e
IMPERFECT					
	ero	avevo	abit**avo**	ripet**evo**	part**ivo**
	eri	avevi	abit**avi**	ripet**evi**	part**ivi**
	era	aveva	abit**ava**	ripet**eva**	part**iva**
	eravamo	avevamo	abit**avamo**	ripet**evamo**	part**ivamo**
	eravate	avevate	abit**avate**	ripet**evate**	part**ivate**
	erano	avevano	abit**avano**	ripet**evano**	part**ivano**
PLUPERFECT					
	ero stato/a	avevo avuto	avevo abit**ato**	avevo ripet**uto**	ero part**ito/a**
	eri stato/a	avevi avuto	avevi abitato	avevi ripetuto	eri partito/a
	era stato/a	aveva avuto	aveva abitato	aveva ripetuto	era partito/a
	eravamo stati/e	avevamo avuto	avevamo abitato	avevamo ripetuto	eravamo partiti/e
	eravate stati/e	avevate avuto	avevate abitato	avevate ripetuto	eravate partiti/e
	erano stati/e	avevano avuto	avevano abitato	avevano ripetuto	erano partiti/e

	ESSERE	AVERE	ABITARE	RIPETERE	PARTIRE
PAST HISTORIC					
	fui	ebbi	abit**ai**	ripet**ei**	part**ii**
	fosti	avesti	abit**asti**	ripet**esti**	part**isti**
	fu	ebbe	abit**ò**	ripet**é**	partì
	fummo	avemmo	abit**ammo**	ripet**emmo**	part**immo**
	foste	aveste	abit**aste**	ripet**este**	part**iste**
	furono	ebbero	abit**arono**	ripet**erono**	part**irono**
PAST ANTERIOR					
	fui stato/a	ebbi avuto	ebbi abit**ato**	ebbi ripet**uto**	fui part**ito/a**
	fosti stato/a	avesti avuto	avesti abitato	avesti ripetuto	fosti partito/a
	fu stato/a	ebbe avuto	ebbe abitato	ebbe ripetuto	fu partito/a
	fummo stati/e	avemmo avuto	avemmo abitato	avemmo ripetuto	fummo partiti/e
	foste stati/e	aveste avuto	aveste abitato	aveste ripetuto	foste partiti/e
	furono stati/e	ebbero avuto	ebbero abitato	ebbero ripetuto	furono partiti/e
FUTURE					
	sarò	avrò	abit**erò**	ripet**erò**	part**irò**
	sarai	avrai	abit**erai**	ripet**erai**	part**irai**
	sarà	avrà	abit**erà**	ripet**erà**	part**irà**
	saremo	avremo	abit**eremo**	ripet**eremo**	part**iremo**
	serete	avrete	abit**erete**	ripet**erete**	part**irete**
	saranno	avranno	abit**eranno**	ripet**eranno**	part**iranno**
FUTURE PERECT					
	sarò stato/a	avrò avuto	avrò abit**ato**	avrò ripet**uto**	sarò part**ito/a**
	sarai stato/a	avrai avuto	avrai abitato	avrai ripetuto	sarai partito/a
	sarà stato/a	avrà avuto	avrà abitato	avrà ripetuto	sarà partito/a
	saremo stati/e	avremo avuto	avremo abitato	avremo ripetuto	saremo partiti/e
	sarete stati/e	avrete avuto	avrete abitato	avrete ripetuto	sarete partiti/e
	saranno stati/e	avranno avuto	avranno abitato	avranno ripetuto	saranno partiti/e

SUBJUNCTIVE (CONGIUNTIVO)

	ESSERE	AVERE	ABITARE	RIPETERE	PARTIRE
PRESENTE					
	sia	abbia	abiti	ripet**a**	part**a**
	sia	abbia	abiti	ripet**a**	part**a**
	sia	abbia	abiti	ripet**a**	part**a**
	siamo	abbiamo	abit**iamo**	ripet**iamo**	part**iamo**
	siate	abbiate	abit**iate**	ripet**iate**	part**iate**
	siano	abbiano	abit**ino**	ripet**ano**	part**ano**
PAST					
	sia stato/a	abbia avuto	abbia abit**ato**	abbia ripet**uto**	sia part**ito/a**
	sia stato/a	abbia avuto	abbia abitato	abbia ripetuto	sia partito/a
	sia stato/a	abbia avuto	abbia abitato	abbia ripetuto	sia partito/a
	siamo stati/e	abbiamo avuto	abbiamo abitato	abbiamo ripetuto	siamo partiti/e
	siate stati/e	abbiate avuto	abbiate abitato	abbiate ripetuto	siate partiti/e
	siano stati/e	abbiano avuto	abbiano abitato	abbiano ripetuto	siano partiti/e
IMPERFECT					
	fossi	avessi	abit**assi**	ripet**essi**	part**issi**
	fossi	avessi	abit**assi**	ripet**essi**	part**issi**
	fosse	avesse	abit**asse**	ripet**esse**	part**isse**
	fossimo	avessimo	abit**assimo**	ripet**essimo**	part**issimo**
	foste	aveste	abit**aste**	ripet**este**	part**iste**
	fossero	avessero	abit**assero**	ripet**essero**	part**issero**
PLUPERFECT					
	fossi stato/a	avessi avuto	avessi abit**ato**	avessi ripet**uto**	fossi part**ito/a**
	fossi stato/a	avessi avuto	avessi abitato	avessi ripetuto	fossi partito/a
	fosse stato/a	avesse avuto	avesse abitato	avesse ripetuto	fosse partito/a
	fossimo stati/e	avessimo avuto	avessimo abitato	avessimo ripetuto	fossimo partiti/e
	foste stati/e	aveste avuto	aveste abitato	aveste ripetuto	foste partiti/e
	fossero stati/e	avessero avuto	avessero abitato	avessero ripetuto	fossero partiti/e

CONDITIONAL (CONDIZIONALE)

PRESENT	sarei	avrei	abit**erei**	ripet**erei**	part**irei**
	saresti	avresti	abit**eresti**	ripet**eresti**	part**iresti**
	sarebbe	avrebbe	abit**erebbe**	ripet**erebbe**	part**irebbe**
	saremmo	avremmo	abit**eremmo**	ripet**eremmo**	part**iremmo**
	sareste	avreste	abit**ereste**	ripet**ereste**	part**ireste**
	sarebbero	avrebbero	abit**erebbero**	ripet**erebbero**	part**irebbero**
PAST	sarei stato/a	avrei avuto	avrei abit**ato**	avrei ripet**uto**	sarei part**ito/a**
	saresti stato/a	avresti avuto	avresti abitato	avresti ripetuto	saresti partito/a
	sarebbe stato/a	avrebbe avuto	avrebbe abitato	avrebbe ripetuto	sarebbe partito/a
	saremmo stati/e	avremmo avuto	avremmo abitato	avremmo ripetuto	saremmo partiti/e
	sareste stati/e	avreste avuto	avreste abitato	avreste ripetuto	sareste partiti/e
	sarebbero stati/e	avrebbero avuto	avrebbero abitato	avrebbero ripetuto	sarebbero partiti/e

IMPERATIVE (IMPERATIVO)

sii (tu)	abbi	abit**a**	ripet**i**	part**i**
sia (Lei)	abbia	abit**i**	ripet**a**	part**a**
siamo (noi)	abbiamo	abit**iamo**	ripet**iamo**	part**iamo**
siate (voi)	abbiate	abit**ate**	ripet**ete**	part**ite**
siano (Loro)	abbiano	abit**ino**	ripet**ano**	part**ano**

GERUND (GERUNDIO)

PRESENT	essendo	avendo	abit**ando**	ripet**endo**	part**endo**
PAST	essendo stato/a/i/e	avendo avuto	avendo abitato	avendo ripetuto	essendo partito/a/i/e

PARTICIPLE (PARTICIPIO)

PRESENT	(essente)	avente	abit**ante**	ripet**ente**	part**ente**
PAST	stato/a/i/e	avuto	abit**ato**	ripet**uto**	part**ito**

INFINITIVE (INFINITO)

PRESENT	essere	avere	abit**are**	ripet**ere**	part**ire**
PERFECT	essere stato/a/i/e	avere avuto	avere abitato	avere ripetuto	essere partito/a/i/e

INDEX

References given are to Section Numbers

Abbreviations used in the index:
adj. adjective
adv. adverb
conj. conjunction
pron. pronoun

Index